Building Scales, Chords, and Arpeggios

The Workbook, No. 2
from Maestro Music Methods
By: Beth Secrist & Joshua Zabatta

Thank you for purchasing **THE WORKBOOK, No. 2: BUILDING SCALES, CHORDS, AND ARPEGGIOS**. This book was created following the circle of fifths. The materials in this book can be used in whatever order the student or teacher see fit. The following skills are addressed in this workbook.

12-Bar Blues Pattern
Augmented Arpeggios
Blues Chord Progressions
Blues Scales
Cadence Pattern
Chord Inversions
Circle of Fifths
Diminished Arpeggios
Dominant 7 Arpeggios
Harmonic Minor Scales
Key Signatures
Major Arpeggios
Major Scales
Melodic Minor Scales
Minor Arpeggios
Natural Minor Scales
Parallel/Relative Minors
Root Position Chords
Writing Scales, Chords, and Cadences on the Staff

REVIEW: GEOGRAPHY OF THE KEYBOARD AND THE STAFF

You'll see below that every key on the keyboard has a name and its own place. The keys also line up with their own note on the staff. Note that C4 is middle C.

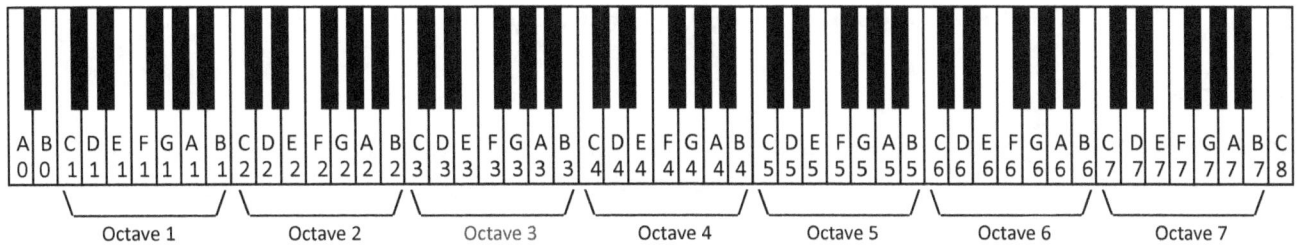

See below how notes on the staff line up on the piano. Middle C (or C4) is one ledger line above on the Bass Clef or one ledger line below on the Treble Clef.

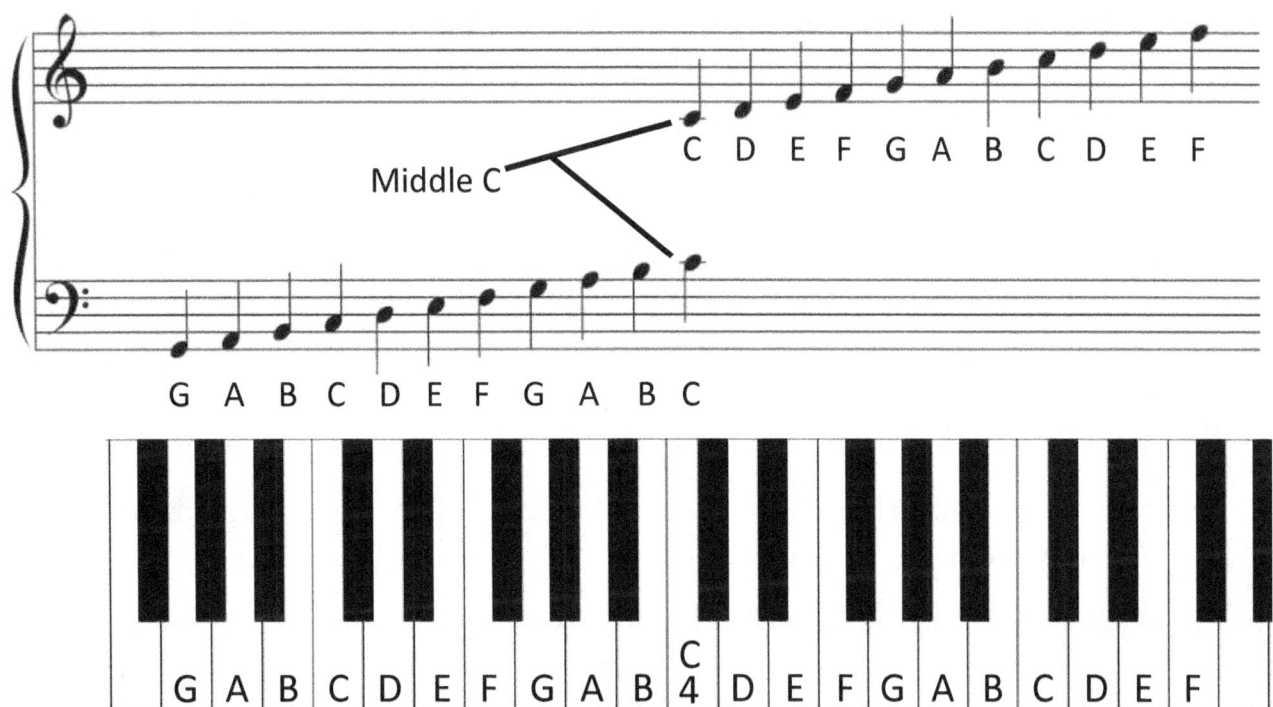

Lines & Spaces on the Treble Clef

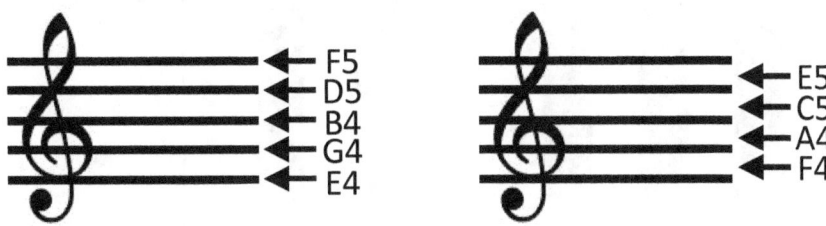

Lines & Spaces on the Bass Clef

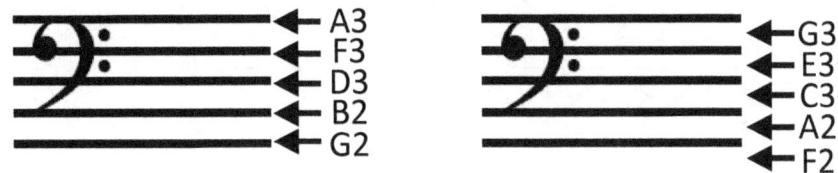

How Scales Work

As we covered in The Workbook, No. 1, a scale is a group of notes following an organized pattern, going up and down. The notes are grouped based on the spaces between them. In our major and minor scales, notes are organized by half steps and whole steps.

Half Step:
To move a half step up or down on the piano, you'll go to the very next key, no matter the color. In the picture, you can see a half step when going from "E" to "F" because there are no keys between them.

Whole Step:
An easy way to remember a whole step is that there will be one "whole" key in between the two notes. In the picture below, there is a black key in between the "C" and the "D." A whole step is also made up of two half steps.

Major Scales (1 Octave)

The Major Scale starts with the same pattern of whole steps and half steps as that of the 5-finger Major Scale. However, you will ascend to the eighth scale degree instead of the fifth. The Major Scale pattern goes as follows:

Whole-Whole-Half-Whole-Whole-Whole-Half

Below is a picture of how this looks on a C Major Scale. Notice that the 1-octave scale begins and ends on the same note (in this case, C). Work with your teacher to discuss the best fingering when practicing Major Scales.

C Major Scale

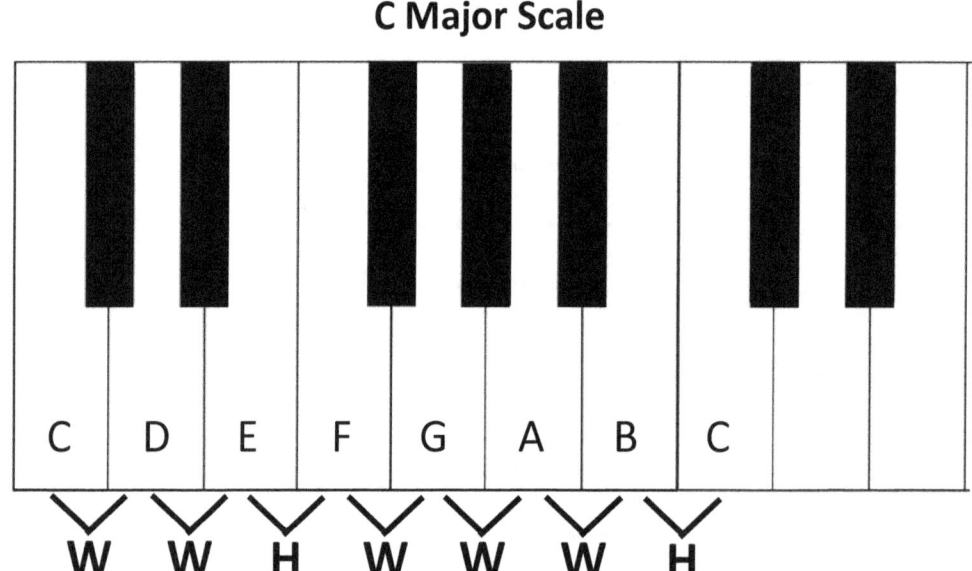

Minor Scales (1 Octave)

There are 3 types of minor scales. The notes of the first five scale degrees of each one are actually the same as the minor 5-finger scales learned in Book 1. You can find the minor scale in a couple of different ways. From a major scale, you can find the relative minor scale or the parallel minor scale. We'll show you how to find the parallel minor scales here. Relative minor will be addressed later in the book.

Natural Minor Scale

The natural minor scale can be found by lowering the 3rd, 6th, and 7th scale degrees of the major scale by a half step. If you look at C Major, that means we would lower the E, A, and B by a half step. Notice that this also changes our pattern of whole steps and half steps.

Whole-Half-Whole-Whole-Half-Whole-Whole

To the right is how this looks after C Major is changed to become C Natural Minor. Notice there is now an E Flat, A Flat, and B Flat.

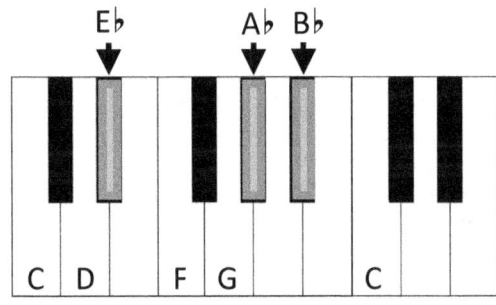

Harmonic Minor Scale

The Harmonic Minor Scale is very similar to Natural Minor. The only difference is that the 7th degree of the scale stays raised. This creates a unique sound at the top of the scale, because there is a slightly larger space between the 6th and 7th scale degrees. In C Harmonic Minor, notice that we have a B instead of a B Flat near the top of the scale.

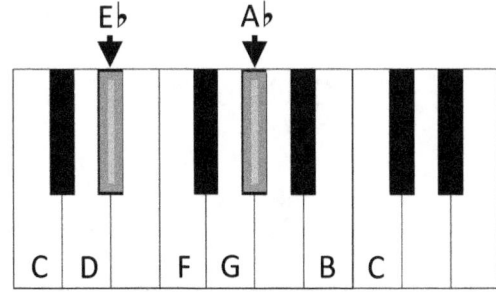

Melodic Minor Scale

The Melodic Minor Scale is very unique in that the notes are different ascending (going up) than they are descending (going down). The first 5 notes are the same as any other minor scale. However, the 6th and 7th notes going up stay raised just like in a Major scale. Then while descending, the notes are exactly the same as in the Natural Minor Scale. There's a saying that will help in remembering this scale. "First, it's minor. Then it's Major. Then it's minor all the way down." One can even sing the notes of the scale while reciting those words.

C Melodic Minor (Ascending)   **C Melodic Minor (Descending)**

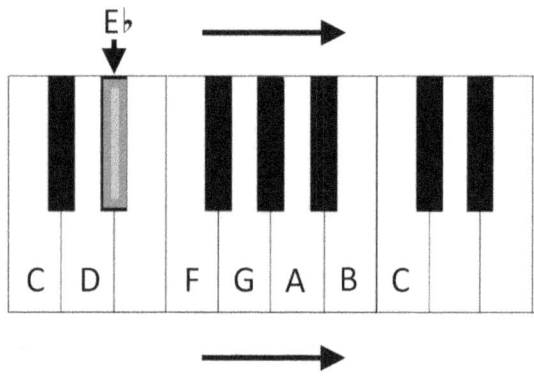 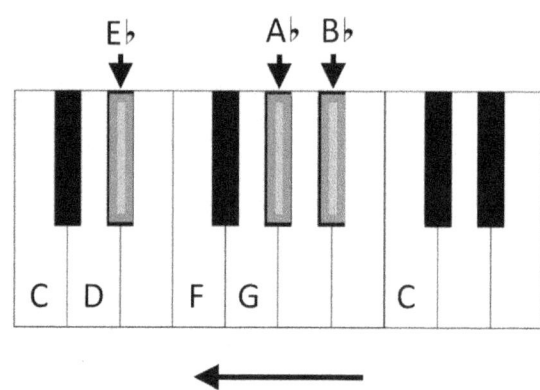

Key Signatures

The **Key Signature** is a group of flat signs or sharp signs that let us know which notes to raise or lower in the music. The key signature generally appears immediately after the clef in music but can show up in other places as well. It can be helpful because it keeps the composer of a piece from needing to continuously write in accidentals. For example, we just learned how to create a C natural minor scale (which contains B Flat, E Flat, and A Flat). A song in the key of C minor doesn't need flat signs in every measure, because the composer includes them in the key signature. The performer then knows to play them throughout the piece automatically.

C Major (*No # or ♭ signs*)   **C Minor** (*3 ♭ signs*)

Root Position Chords (Triads)

For this exercise in the workbook, the student will learn to write root position chords for each step of the scale. These will be written out as triads. A Triad is a three-note chord. You most likely came across these when you learned major and minor arpeggios in Workbook 1. However, instead of playing the notes separately, here you'll play them together in harmony (also called blocked chords).

How Triads Are Built

The Triad is made up of 3 notes that are stacked upon each other. The bottom note is called the ROOT. The next stacked note will be a Third above it, and is therefore called the THIRD. The last note is stacked another Third above the middle note, and is called the FIFTH. It's called the Fifth, because it is a fifth above our Root. The giveaway that a chord is a Triad is when all Line Notes stacked on each other or all Space Notes stacked on each other.

Triad Made of Line Notes

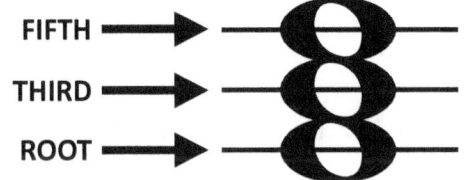

Triad Made of Space Notes

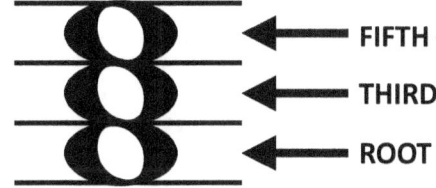

Triads on the Major Scale

Below are the triads as demonstrated in C Major. The notes of the chord are listed above with the roots in **BOLD**. The Roman Numerals below indicate the scale degree and the quality of the chord. Upper Case Roman Numerals tell us the chord is major, while lower case roman numerals show that the chord is minor or diminished (in the case of the 7th chord with the o next to it. **Note:** In other keys with sharps or flats, the letter name skips will always remain consistent. Be sure to apply the accidentals in that key signature.

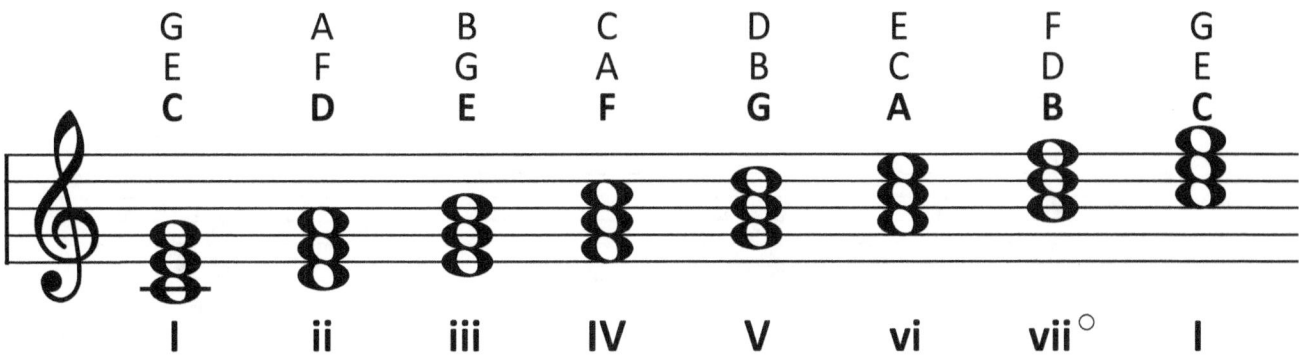

Cadence

A Cadence is a progression or order of chords that helps move the music forward. From our root position chords exercise, we'll be using the I, IV, V, and V7 chords. You'll see below that the V7 chord adds one more third on top. Most times when you practice these, you'll play the chord in the right hand and the root in the left hand.

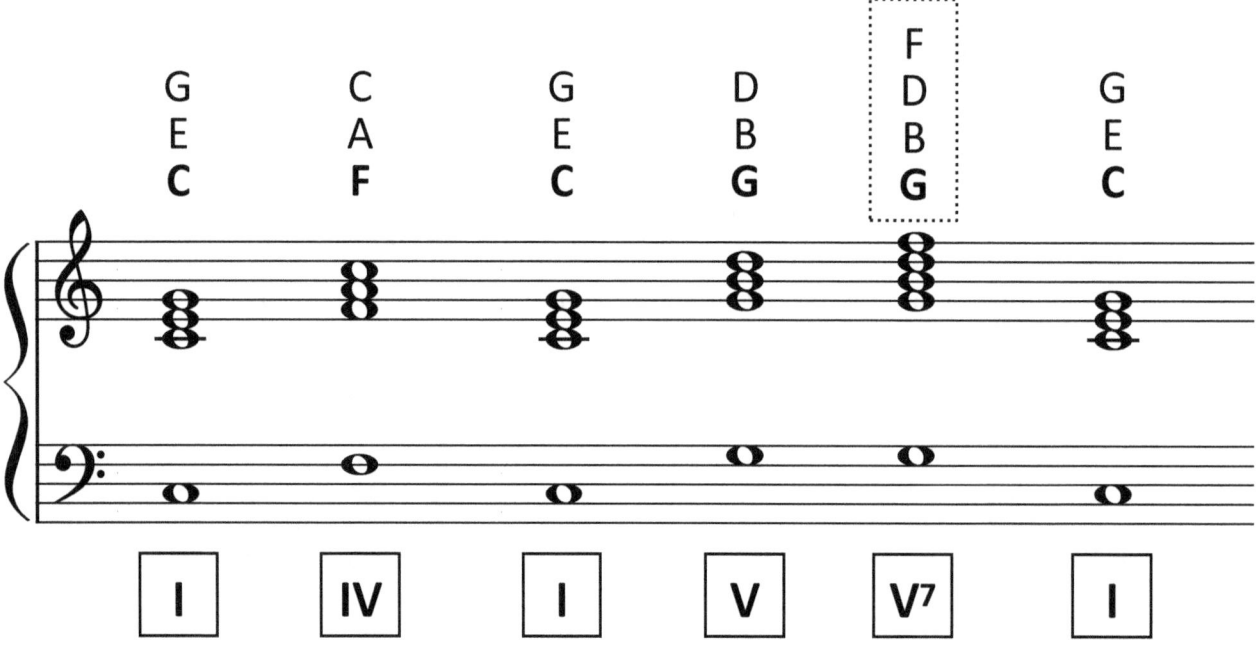

Cadence Using Inversions & Common Tones

When the cadence is taught, teachers often times have students practice it using inversions. An inversion is when we rearrange notes using the same letter names from the root position chord. This makes playing the chords easier with fewer jumps. Below, you will see the same cadence as above using inversions. Look for the common tones between the chords. Which ones change? Which ones stay the same?

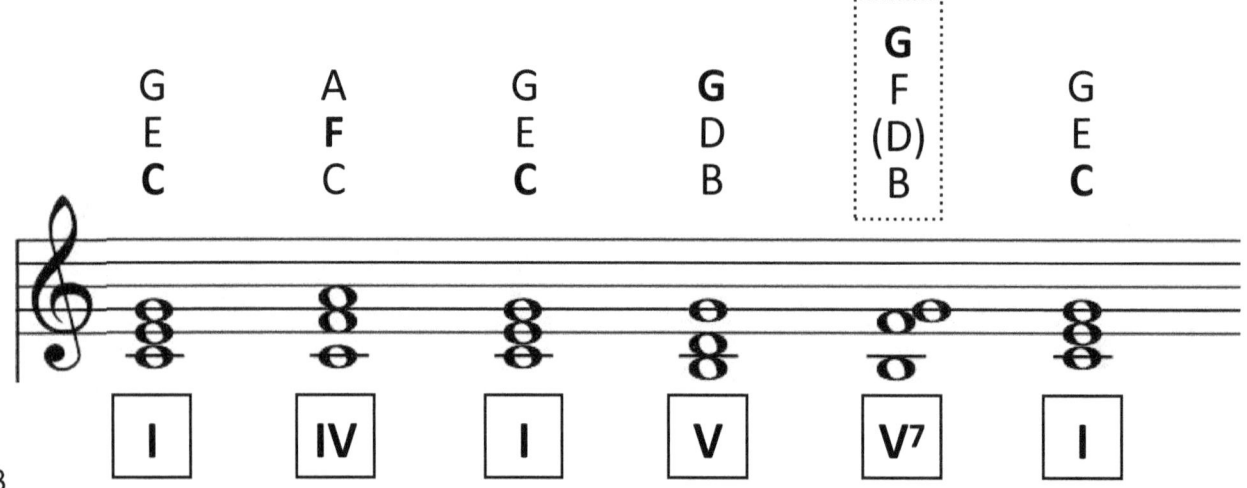

The Blues Scale

As the name implies, The Blues Scale is a pattern of notes that creates a distinctly "bluesy" sound. It's basically a minor pentatonic scale (5-Note Scale) with an added "Blue Note," which gives it its unique sound. The Blue Note is a Flat Five (the 5th scale degree lowered by a half step). The Blues Scale is used mainly in Jazz and Blues music, but it can be found in other styles as well. The pattern for this scale is shown below.

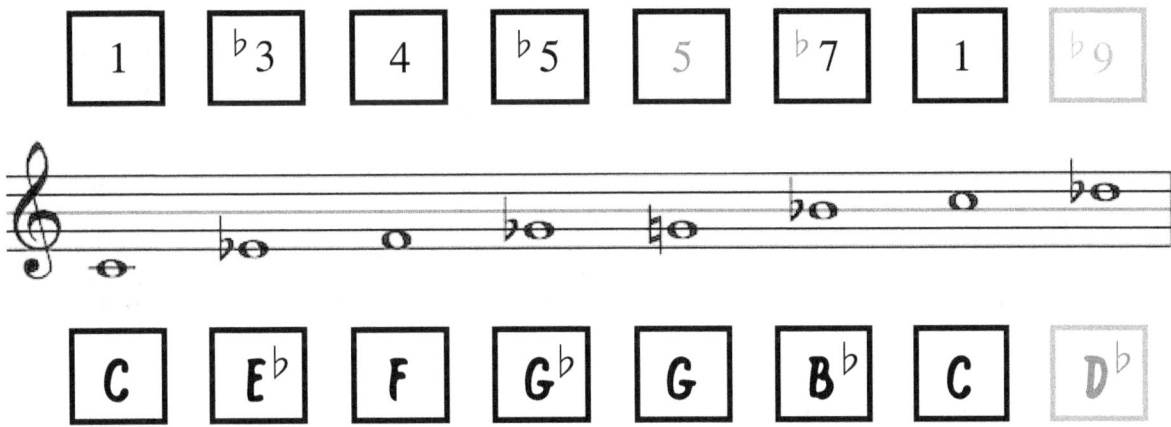

Work with your teacher to understand and hear the distinct sound of the Blues Scale. You may notice there's an optional added note at the top of the scale. This note is the flat 9, and it is located one half-step past the octave. You may play this when practicing if you like or you can stop at the octave before descending.

Blues Progression (ii-V-I)

The 2-5-1 progression is commonly found in jazz and blues music, but it's also used in pop, rock, classical, and other styles. Knowing how this works and practicing it will improve your playing, no matter what kind of music you try. Below is how it looks first using root position chords and then an option using inversions.

9

12-Bar Blues

The 12-bar Blues is a pattern of chords used over twelve measures in a piece. It uses the I, IV, and V Chords. The pattern is included in each key, allowing you to explore playing.

One-Octave Arpeggios Sharing Tonic

An Arpeggio is an arrangement of notes in a chord played harp-like. They are usually played starting with the lowest note, covering each note in the chord from lowest to highest and back. The most prominent chords and arpeggios are presented in every key of this book.

Composition Sections

Every key in this book features a one-page section dedicated entirely to composition. You may use this to explore writing music in every key. You may also use the staff paper to write out exercises.

"Happy Birthday" In Each Key

As a fun side activity, the song "Happy Birthday" is presented with Lead Sheets in every key in this book. What better way to familiarize yourself with each key?

The Circle of Fifths

In this book, we present the scales & arpeggios following the pattern in the Circle of Fifths. We start with C and go clockwise to C Sharp. Then we continue with F and go counter-clockwise to G Flat. You may learn the scales & arpeggios in whatever order you'd like.

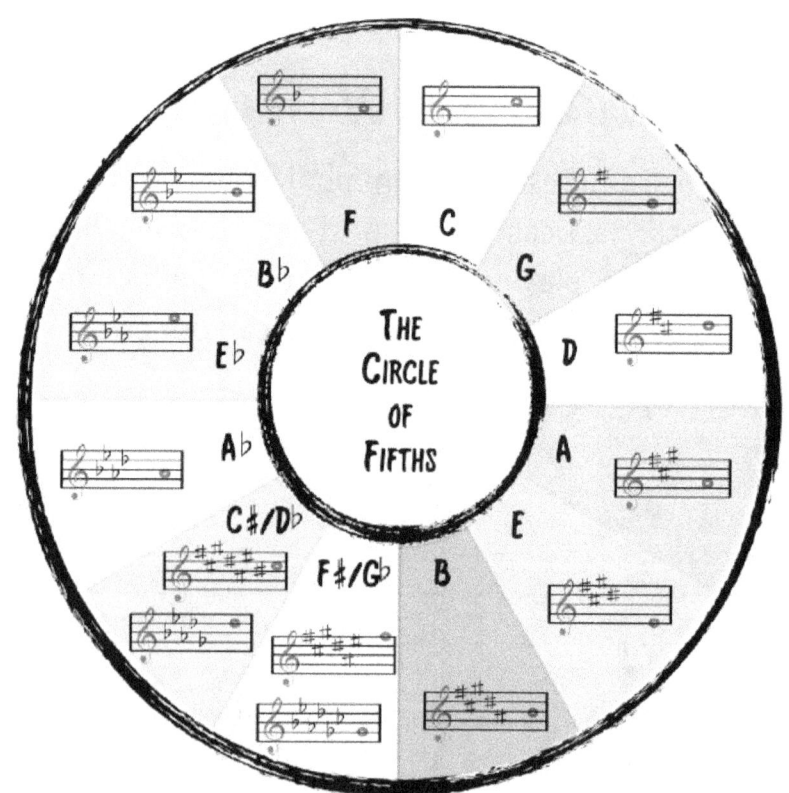

TERMS & DEFINITIONS

We've covered the majority of what you'll need to know as you read and work through this book. However, here are some more terms that will be helpful. Return to this section whenever you need a review.

Scale: A pattern or arrangement of notes in a particular order.

Scale Degrees: The names and numbers of each note in a scale

Arpeggio: The arrangement of notes in a chord played harp-like. (Often times, starting with the lowest note and playing each note in the chord from lowest to highest and back)

Chord: Three or more notes played at the same time.

Sharp: Raise the note by 1/2 step

Flat: Lower the note by 1/2 step

Natural: Cancels a sharp or flat

Double Sharp: Raises the note by a whole step

Double Flat: Lowers the note by a whole step

Circle of Fifths: The succession of keys proceeding in intervals of fifths, either ascending or descending.

Key Signature: The sharps or flats written on the staff that indicate the key or scale the piece is based on.

Inversion: The rearrangement of notes in a chord using the same letter names. I.e., C-Chord in root position= C-E-G. In the first inversion, put the C on top of the chord so that E is now on the bottom: E-G-C. For second inversion, put C in the middle and G on the bottom: G-C-E.

C MAJOR

Major Scale Pattern: W-W-H-W-W-W-H

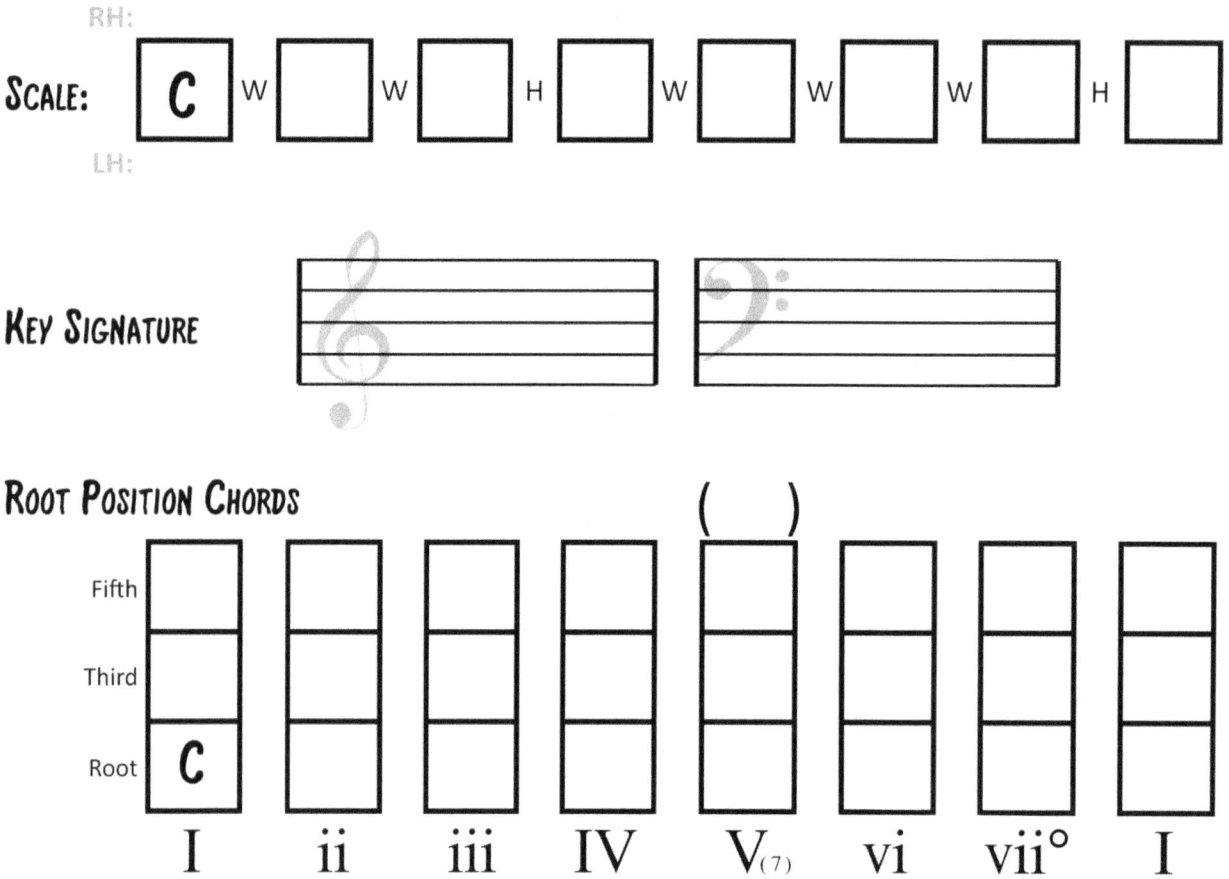

Suggested Practice for Root Position Chords:
1. Block the Chord using fingers 1, 3, and 5.
2. Name the chord.
3. Arpeggiate the chord (cross-hand arpeggios).

Cadence

Suggested Practice:
1. Play chords in the RH and play roots in the LH.
2. Try playing the cadence with different rhythms.
3. The cadence can be played as root position chords or by going chord to chord sharing common tones (inversions).

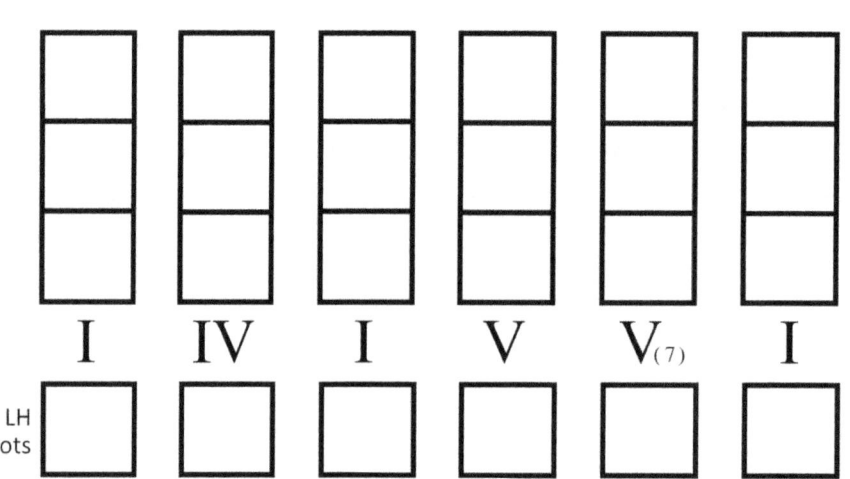

Major Scale written on the Staff

Root Position Chords Written on the Staff

Cadence Written on the Staff

C MAJOR

BLUES SCALE:

RH:

☐ ☐ ☐ ☐ ☐ ☐ ☐ ☐ (OPTIONAL)

1 b3 4 b5 5 b7 1 b9

LH:

BLUES PROGRESSION:

ii V I

12-BAR BLUES PATTERN:

1) Four Measures of the I Chord.
2) Two Measures of the IV Chord.
3) Two Measures of the I Chord.
4) One Measure of the V Chord.
5) One Measure of the IV Chord.
6) Two Measures of the I Chord.

*You can try this with full chords or play just the root and fifth with your left hand while you improvise a melody from the blues scale with your right hand.

OCTAVE ARPEGGIOS SHARING TONIC

Major:
Write in the Root, 3rd, 5th, and octave of the Major Scale.

☐ ☐ ☐ ☐

Augmented:
From Major, Raise 5th by a 1/2 step.

☐ ☐ ☐ ☐

Minor:
From Major, Lower 3rd by a 1/2 step.

☐ ☐ ☐ ☐

Diminished 7th:
From Major, Lower 3rd & 5th by a 1/2 step, and Lower 7th by a whole step.

☐ ☐ ☐ ☐ ☐

Dominant 7th:
From Major, Lower 7th by a 1/2 step.

☐ ☐ ☐ ☐ ☐

Blues Scale written on the Staff

Blues Progression written on the Staff

"Happy Birthday" in the key of C (with Lead Sheet)

Parallel Minor Scales in C

Natural:
From Major, lower the 3rd, 6th & 7th by a 1/2 step

RH:
| C | W | | H | | W | | W | | H | | W | | W | |

LH:

Natural Minor Scale written on the Staff

Key Signature

Harmonic:
From Natural Minor, raise the 7th back up a 1/2 step.

RH:
LH:

Melodic:
Ascending: From Major, lower the 3rd. Descending: Same as Natural Minor.

RH:
LH:

RH:
LH:

Explore: Composition in C

G MAJOR

Major Scale Pattern: W-W-H-W-W-W-H

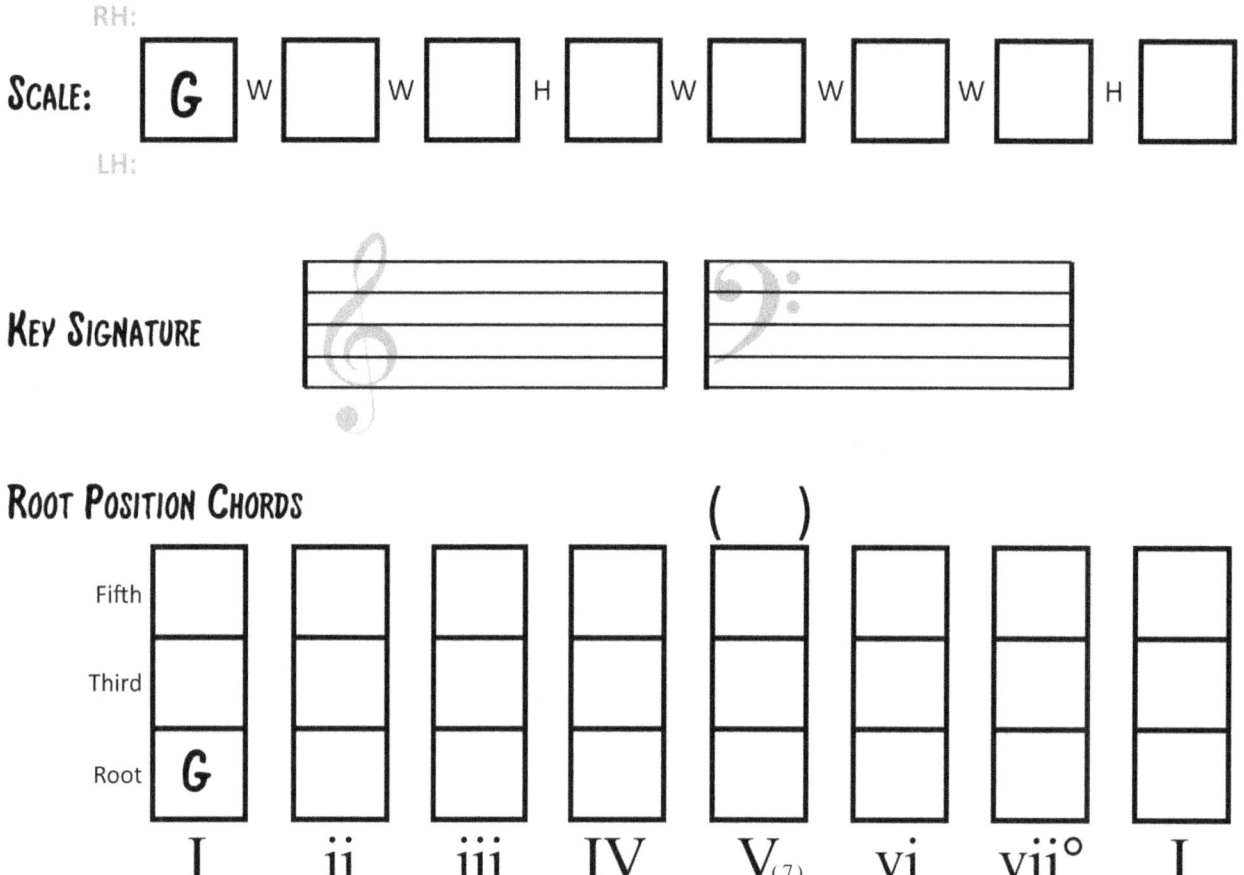

Suggested Practice for Root Position Chords:
1. Block the Chord using fingers 1, 3, and 5.
2. Name the chord.
3. Arpeggiate the chord (cross-hand arpeggios).

Cadence

Suggested Practice:
1. Play chords in the RH and play roots in the LH.
2. Try playing the cadence with different rhythms.
3. The cadence can be played as root position chords or by going chord to chord sharing common tones (inversions).

Major Scale Written on the Staff

Root Position Chords Written on the Staff

Cadence Written on the Staff

G MAJOR

BLUES SCALE:
(OPTIONAL)

RH:

| 1 | b3 | 4 | b5 | 5 | b7 | 1 | b9 |

LH:

BLUES PROGRESSION:

ii   V   I

12-BAR BLUES PATTERN:

1) Four Measures of the I Chord.
2) Two Measures of the IV Chord.
3) Two Measures of the I Chord.
4) One Measure of the V Chord.
5) One Measure of the IV Chord.
6) Two Measures of the I Chord.

*You can try this with full chords or play just the root and fifth with your left hand while you improvise a melody from the blues scale with your right hand.

Octave Arpeggios Sharing Tonic

Major:
Write in the Root, 3rd, 5th, and octave of the Major Scale.

Augmented:
From Major, Raise 5th by a 1/2 step.

Minor:
From Major, Lower 3rd by a 1/2 step.

Diminished 7th:
From Major, Lower 3rd & 5th by a 1/2 step, and Lower 7th by a whole step.

Dominant 7th:
From Major, Lower 7th by a 1/2 step.

Blues Scale written on the Staff

Blues Progression written on the Staff

"Happy Birthday" in the key of G (with Lead Sheet)

21

Parallel Minor Scales in G

Natural:
From Major, lower the 3rd, 6th & 7th by a 1/2 step

RH: | G | W | | H | | W | | W | | H | | W | | W |
LH:

Natural Minor Scale written on the Staff

Key Signature

Harmonic:
From Natural Minor, raise the 7th back up a 1/2 step.

RH:
LH:

Melodic:
Ascending: From Major, lower the 3rd. Descending: Same as Natural Minor.

RH:
LH:

RH:
LH:

Explore: Composition in G

D MAJOR

Major Scale Pattern: W-W-H-W-W-W-H

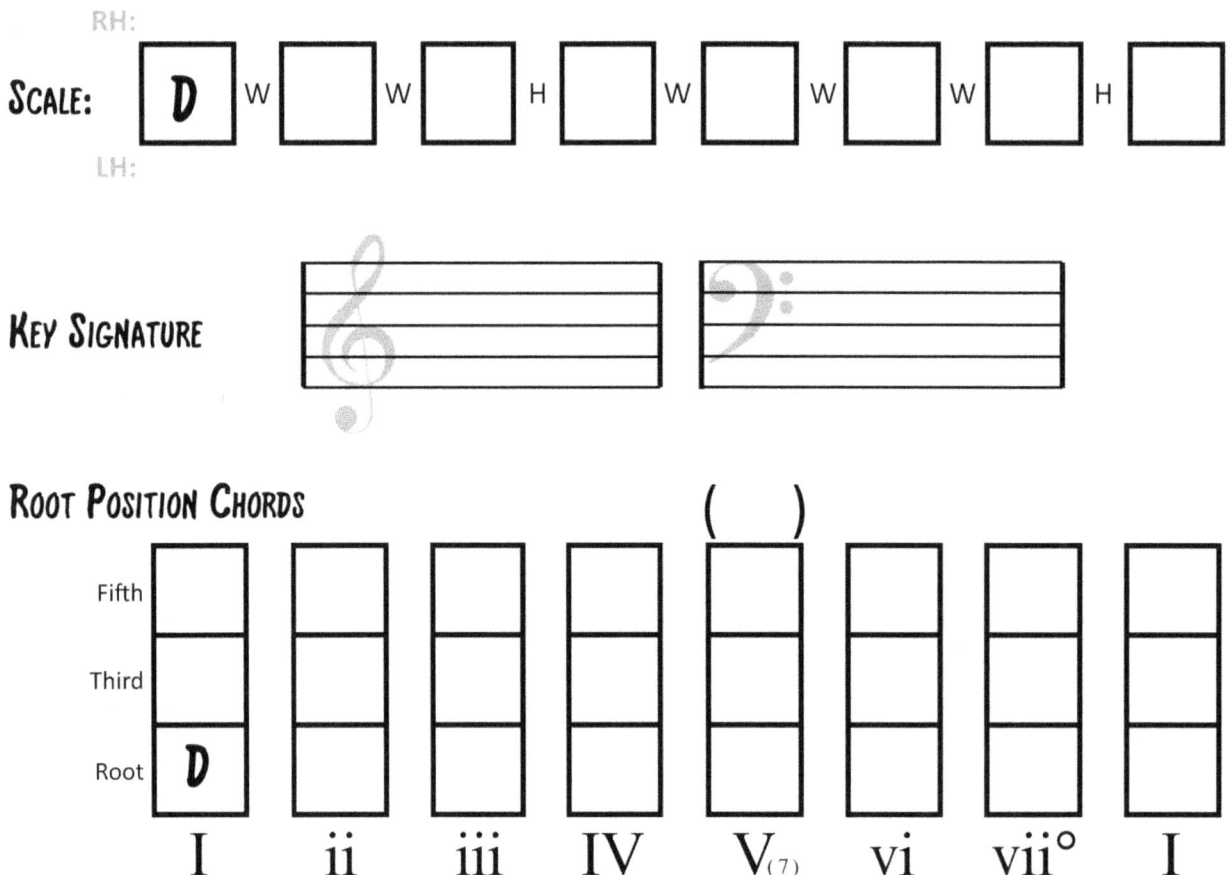

24

Major Scale written on the Staff

Root Position Chords Written on the Staff

Cadence Written on the Staff

D MAJOR

BLUES SCALE:

RH:

☐ ☐ ☐ ☐ ☐ ☐ ☐ ☐ (OPTIONAL)

1 b3 4 b5 5 b7 1 b9

LH:

BLUES PROGRESSION:

ii   V   I

12-BAR BLUES PATTERN:

1) Four Measures of the I Chord.
2) Two Measures of the IV Chord.
3) Two Measures of the I Chord.
4) One Measure of the V Chord.
5) One Measure of the IV Chord.
6) Two Measures of the I Chord.

*You can try this with full chords or play just the root and fifth with your left hand while you improvise a melody from the blues scale with your right hand.

OCTAVE ARPEGGIOS SHARING TONIC

Major:
Write in the Root, 3rd, 5th, and octave of the Major Scale.

☐ ☐ ☐ ☐

Augmented:
From Major, Raise 5th by a 1/2 step.

☐ ☐ ☐ ☐

Minor:
From Major, Lower 3rd by a 1/2 step.

☐ ☐ ☐ ☐

Diminished 7th:
From Major, Lower 3rd & 5th by a 1/2 step, and Lower 7th by a whole step.

☐ ☐ ☐ ☐ ☐

Dominant 7th:
From Major, Lower 7th by a 1/2 step.

☐ ☐ ☐ ☐ ☐

Blues Scale written on the Staff

Blues Progression written on the Staff

"Happy Birthday" in the Key of D (with Lead Sheet)

Parallel Minor Scales in D

Natural:
From Major, lower the 3rd, 6th & 7th by a 1/2 step

RH: | D | W | | H | W | | W | | H | W | | W |
LH:

Natural Minor Scale written on the Staff

Key Signature

Harmonic:
From Natural Minor, raise the 7th back up a 1/2 step.

RH:
LH:

Melodic:
Ascending: From Major, lower the 3rd. Descending: Same as Natural Minor.

RH:
LH:

RH:
LH:

28

Explore: Composition in D

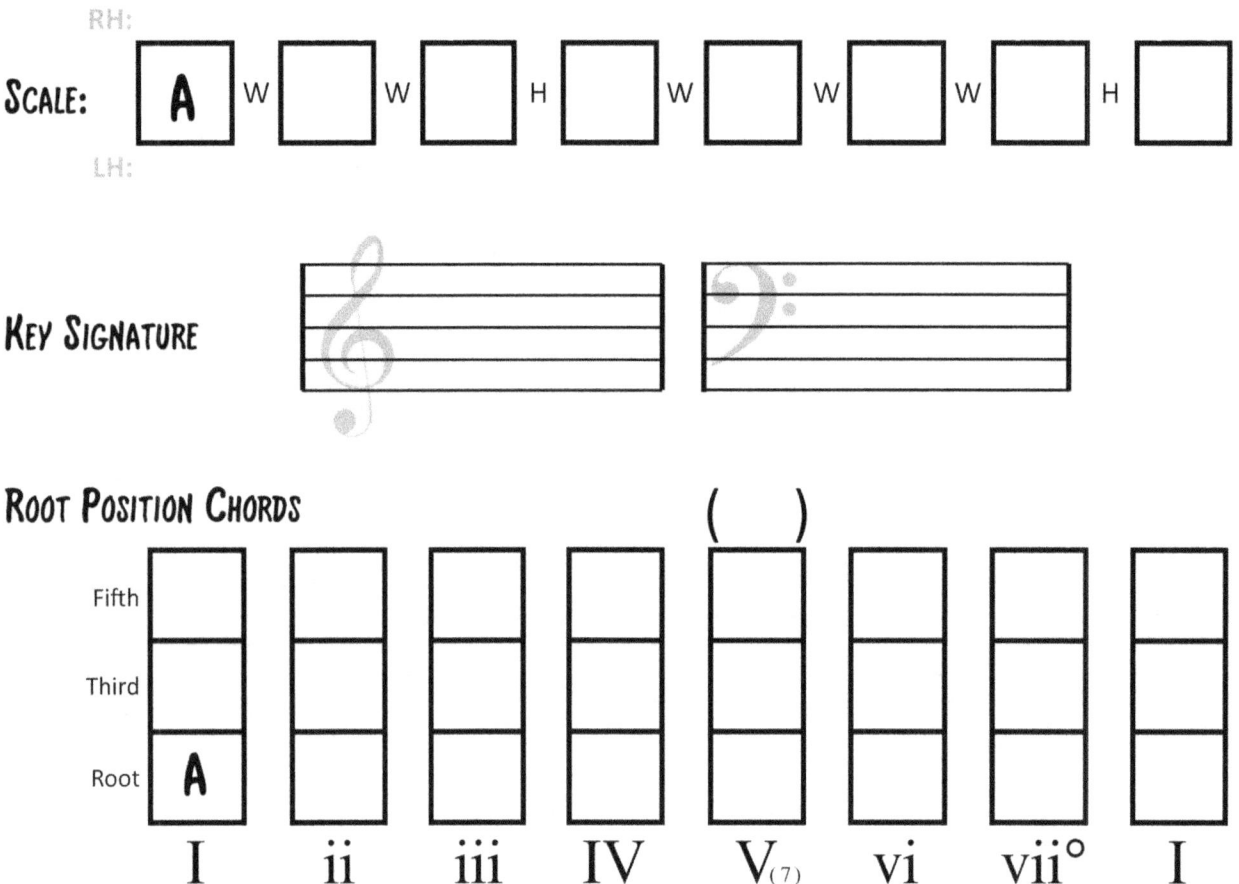

Major Scale written on the Staff

Root Position Chords Written on the Staff

Cadence Written on the Staff

A MAJOR

BLUES SCALE: (OPTIONAL)

RH:

☐ ☐ ☐ ☐ ☐ ☐ ☐ ☐
1 b3 4 b5 5 b7 1 b9

LH:

BLUES PROGRESSION:

ii V I

12-BAR BLUES PATTERN:

1) Four Measures of the I Chord.
2) Two Measures of the IV Chord.
3) Two Measures of the I Chord.
4) One Measure of the V Chord.
5) One Measure of the IV Chord.
6) Two Measures of the I Chord.

*You can try this with full chords or play just the root and fifth with your left hand while you improvise a melody from the blues scale with your right hand.

Octave Arpeggios Sharing Tonic

Major:
Write in the Root, 3rd, 5th, and octave of the Major Scale.

Augmented:
From Major, Raise 5th by a 1/2 step.

Minor:
From Major, Lower 3rd by a 1/2 step.

Diminished 7th:
From Major, Lower 3rd & 5th by a 1/2 step, and Lower 7th by a whole step.

Dominant 7th:
From Major, Lower 7th by a 1/2 step.

BLUES SCALE WRITTEN ON THE STAFF

BLUES PROGRESSION WRITTEN ON THE STAFF

"HAPPY BIRTHDAY" IN THE KEY OF A (WITH LEAD SHEET)

Parallel Minor Scales in A

Natural:
From Major, lower the 3rd, 6th & 7th by a 1/2 step

RH:

| A | W | | H | | W | | W | | H | | W | | W | |

LH:

Natural Minor Scale written on the Staff

Key Signature

Harmonic:
From Natural Minor, raise the 7th back up a 1/2 step.

RH:

LH:

Melodic:
Ascending: From Major, lower the 3rd. Descending: Same as Natural Minor.

RH:

LH:

RH:

LH:

34

Explore: Composition in A

E MAJOR

Major Scale Pattern: W-W-H-W-W-W-H

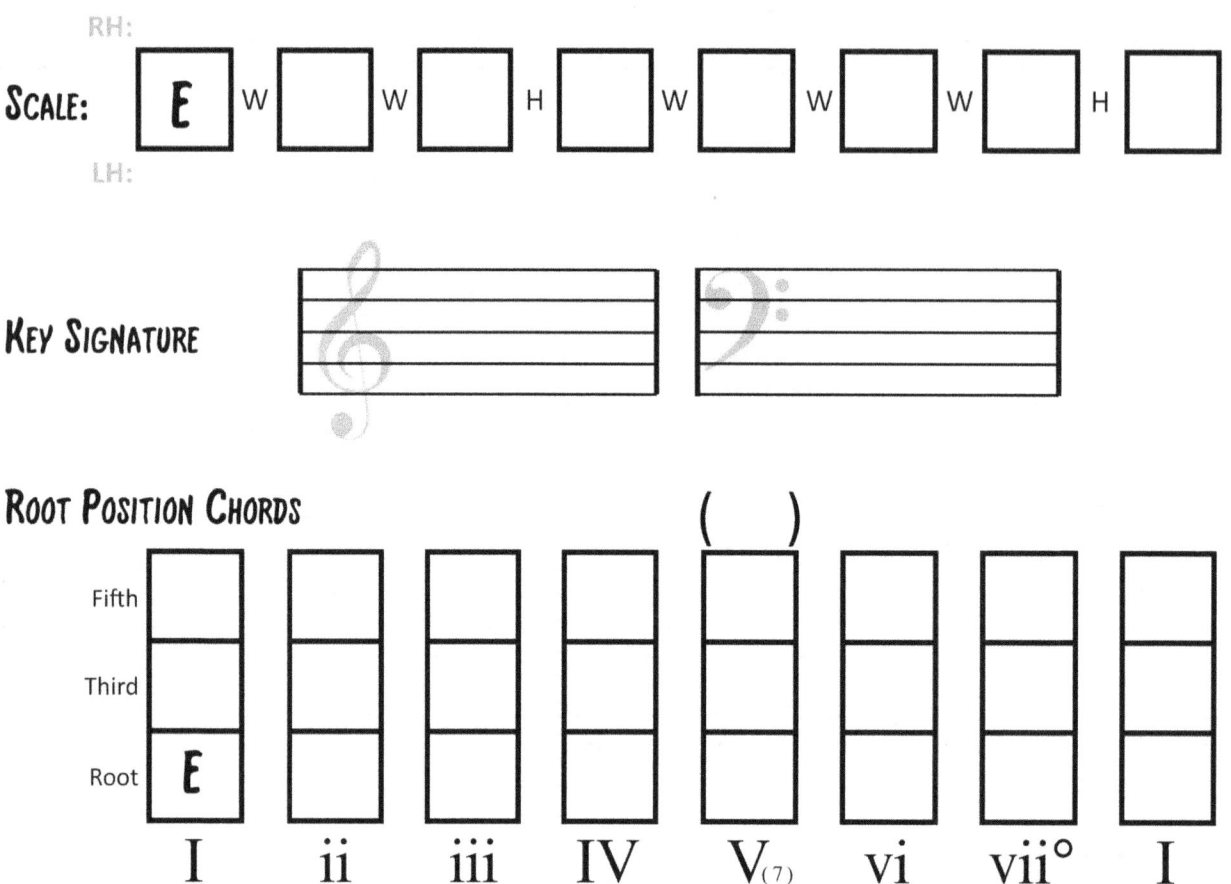

Suggested Practice for Root Position Chords:
1. Block the Chord using fingers 1, 3, and 5.
2. Name the chord.
3. Arpeggiate the chord (cross-hand arpeggios).

CADENCE

Suggested Practice:
1. Play chords in the RH and play roots in the LH.
2. Try playing the cadence with different rhythms.
3. The cadence can be played as root position chords or by going chord to chord sharing common tones (inversions).

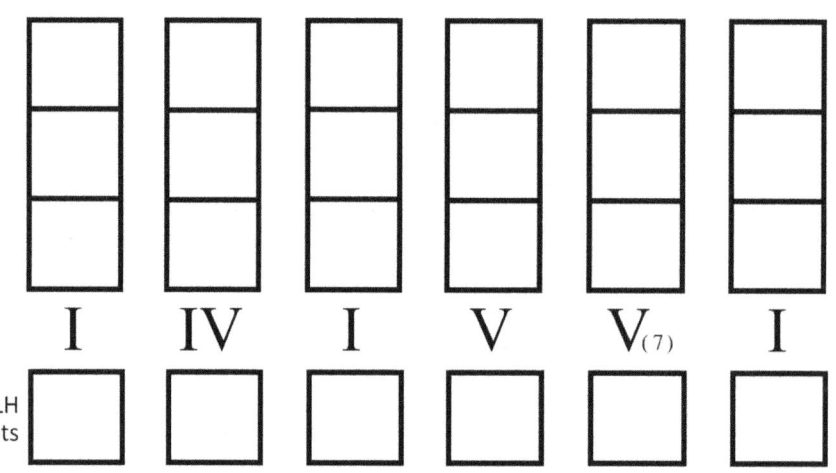

Major Scale written on the Staff

Root Position Chords Written on the Staff

Cadence Written on the Staff

E MAJOR

BLUES SCALE:

RH:

☐ ☐ ☐ ☐ ☐ ☐ ☐ ☐ (OPTIONAL)

1　b3　4　b5　5　b7　1　b9

LH:

BLUES PROGRESSION:

ii　V　I

12-BAR BLUES PATTERN:

1) Four Measures of the I Chord.
2) Two Measures of the IV Chord.
3) Two Measures of the I Chord.
4) One Measure of the V Chord.
5) One Measure of the IV Chord.
6) Two Measures of the I Chord.

*You can try this with full chords or play just the root and fifth with your left hand while you improvise a melody from the blues scale with your right hand.

OCTAVE ARPEGGIOS SHARING TONIC

Major:
Write in the Root, 3rd, 5th, and octave of the Major Scale.

☐ ☐ ☐ ☐

Augmented:
From Major, Raise 5th by a 1/2 step.

☐ ☐ ☐ ☐

Minor:
From Major, Lower 3rd by a 1/2 step.

☐ ☐ ☐ ☐

Diminished 7th:
From Major, Lower 3rd & 5th by a 1/2 step, and Lower 7th by a whole step.

☐ ☐ ☐ ☐ ☐

Dominant 7th:
From Major, Lower 7th by a 1/2 step.

☐ ☐ ☐ ☐ ☐

Blues Scale written on the Staff

Blues Progression written on the Staff

"Happy Birthday" in the key of E (with Lead Sheet)

Parallel Minor Scales in E

Natural:
From Major, lower the 3rd, 6th & 7th by a 1/2 step

RH:
| E | W | | H | | W | | W | | H | | W | | W | |

LH:

Natural Minor Scale written on the Staff

Key Signature

Harmonic:
From Natural Minor, raise the 7th back up a 1/2 step.

RH:
LH:

Melodic:
Ascending: From Major, lower the 3rd. Descending: Same as Natural Minor.

RH:
LH:

RH:
LH:

40

Explore: Composition in E

B MAJOR

Major Scale Pattern: W-W-H-W-W-W-H

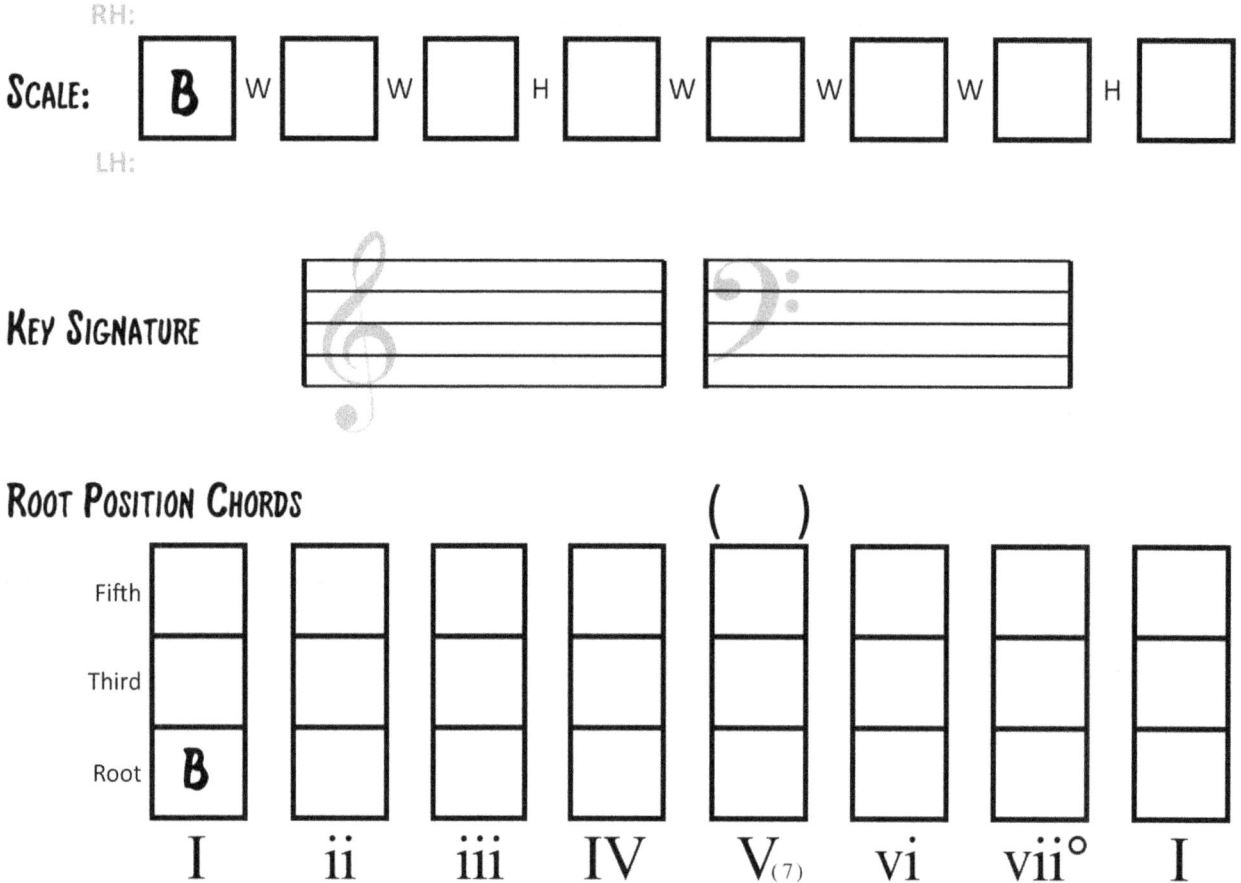

Suggested Practice for Root Position Chords:
1. Block the Chord using fingers 1, 3, and 5.
2. Name the chord.
3. Arpeggiate the chord (cross-hand arpeggios).

Cadence

Suggested Practice:
1. Play chords in the RH and play roots in the LH.
2. Try playing the cadence with different rhythms.
3. The cadence can be played as root position chords or by going chord to chord sharing common tones (inversions).

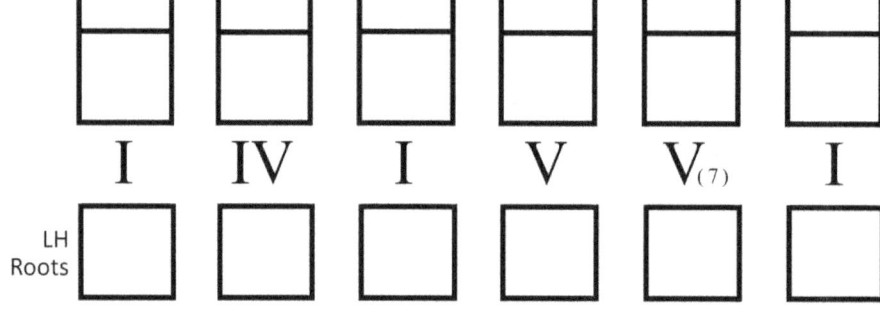

Major Scale written on the Staff

Root Position Chords Written on the Staff

Cadence Written on the Staff

B MAJOR

BLUES SCALE:
(OPTIONAL)

RH:

□ □ □ □ □ □ □ □
1　b3　4　b5　5　b7　1　b9

LH:

BLUES PROGRESSION:

ii　V　I

12-BAR BLUES PATTERN:

1) Four Measures of the I Chord.
2) Two Measures of the IV Chord.
3) Two Measures of the I Chord.
4) One Measure of the V Chord.
5) One Measure of the IV Chord.
6) Two Measures of the I Chord.

*You can try this with full chords or play just the root and fifth with your left hand while you improvise a melody from the blues scale with your right hand.

OCTAVE ARPEGGIOS SHARING TONIC

Major:
Write in the Root, 3rd, 5th, and octave of the Major Scale.

Augmented:
From Major, Raise 5th by a 1/2 step.

Minor:
From Major, Lower 3rd by a 1/2 step.

Diminished 7th:
From Major, Lower 3rd & 5th by a 1/2 step, and Lower 7th by a whole step.

Dominant 7th:
From Major, Lower 7th by a 1/2 step.

BLUES SCALE WRITTEN ON THE STAFF

BLUES PROGRESSION WRITTEN ON THE STAFF

"HAPPY BIRTHDAY" IN THE KEY OF B (WITH LEAD SHEET)

45

Parallel Minor Scales in B

Natural:
From Major, lower the 3rd, 6th & 7th by a 1/2 step

RH:
| B | W | H | W | W | H | W | W |

LH:

Natural Minor Scale written on the Staff

Key Signature

Harmonic:
From Natural Minor, raise the 7th back up a 1/2 step.

RH:
LH:

Melodic:
Ascending: From Major, lower the 3rd. Descending: Same as Natural Minor.

RH:
LH:

RH:
LH:

Explore: Composition in B

F# MAJOR

Major Scale Pattern: W-W-H-W-W-W-H

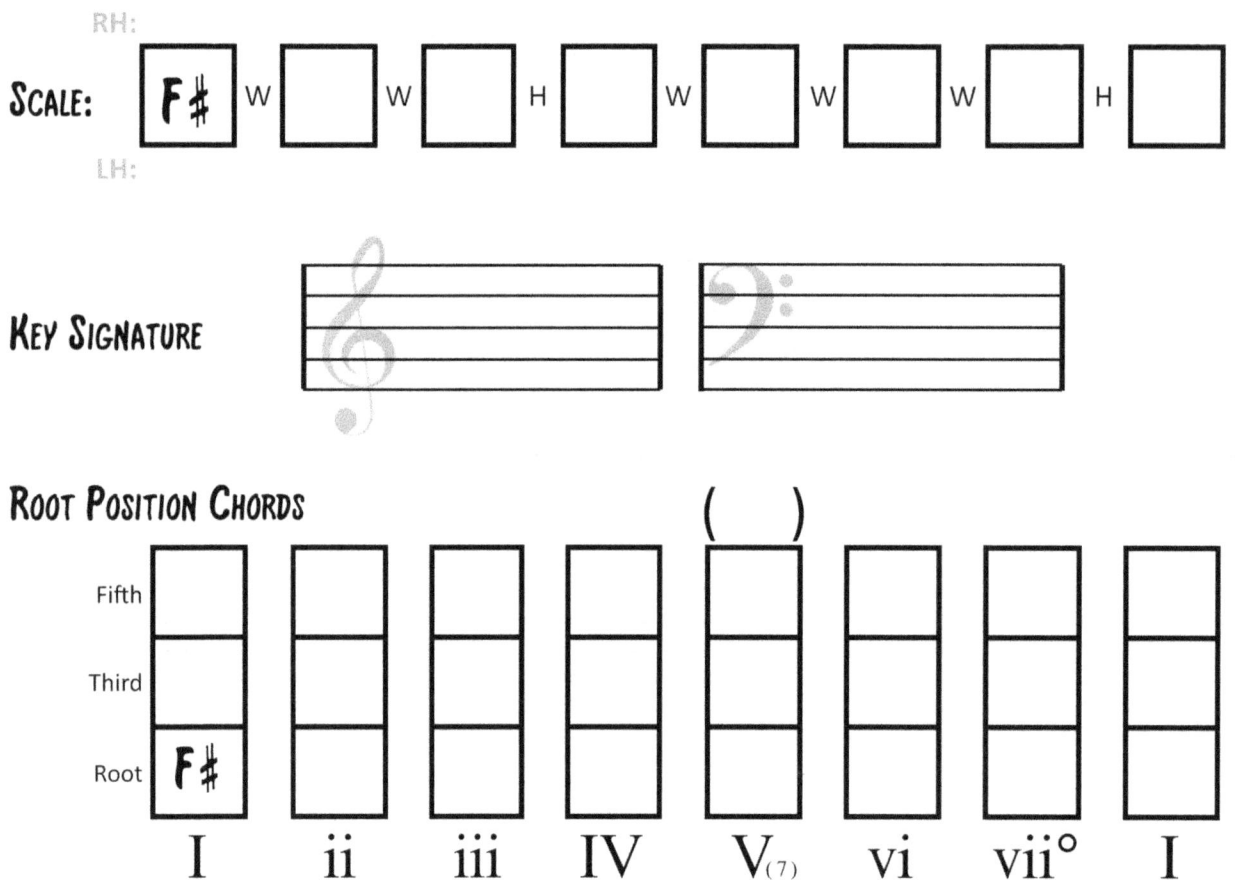

Suggested Practice for Root Position Chords:
1. Block the Chord using fingers 1, 3, and 5.
2. Name the chord.
3. Arpeggiate the chord (cross-hand arpeggios).

CADENCE

Suggested Practice:
1. Play chords in the RH and play roots in the LH.
2. Try playing the cadence with different rhythms.
3. The cadence can be played as root position chords or by going chord to chord sharing common tones (inversions).

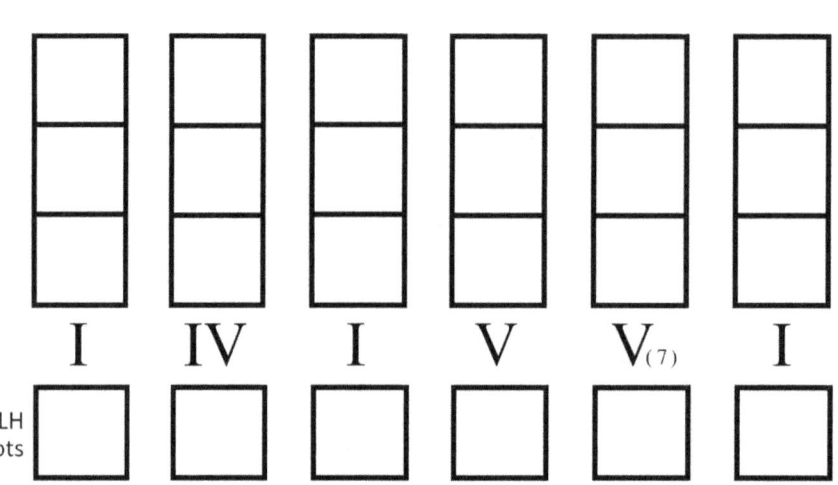

48

Major Scale Written on the Staff

Root Position Chords Written on the Staff

Cadence Written on the Staff

F# MAJOR

BLUES SCALE:

RH:

1 b3 4 b5 5 b7 1 (OPTIONAL) b9

LH:

BLUES PROGRESSION:

ii   V   I

12-BAR BLUES PATTERN:

1) Four Measures of the I Chord.
2) Two Measures of the IV Chord.
3) Two Measures of the I Chord.
4) One Measure of the V Chord.
5) One Measure of the IV Chord.
6) Two Measures of the I Chord.

*You can try this with full chords or play just the root and fifth with your left hand while you improvise a melody from the blues scale with your right hand.

OCTAVE ARPEGGIOS SHARING TONIC

Major:
Write in the Root, 3rd, 5th, and octave of the Major Scale.

Augmented:
From Major, Raise 5th by a 1/2 step.

Minor:
From Major, Lower 3rd by a 1/2 step.

Diminished 7th:
From Major, Lower 3rd & 5th by a 1/2 step, and Lower 7th by a whole step.

Dominant 7th:
From Major, Lower 7th by a 1/2 step.

Blues Scale written on the Staff

Blues Progression written on the Staff

"Happy Birthday" in the key of F♯ (with Lead Sheet)

Parallel Minor Scales in F#

Natural:
From Major, lower the 3rd, 6th & 7th by a 1/2 step

RH:
| F# | W | | H | | W | | W | | W | | H | | W | | W | |

LH:

Natural Minor Scale written on the Staff

Key Signature

Harmonic:
From Natural Minor, raise the 7th back up a 1/2 step.

RH:
LH:

Melodic:
Ascending: From Major, lower the 3rd. Descending: Same as Natural Minor.

RH:
LH:

RH:
LH:

52

Explore: Composition in F#

C# Major

Major Scale Pattern: W-W-H-W-W-W-H

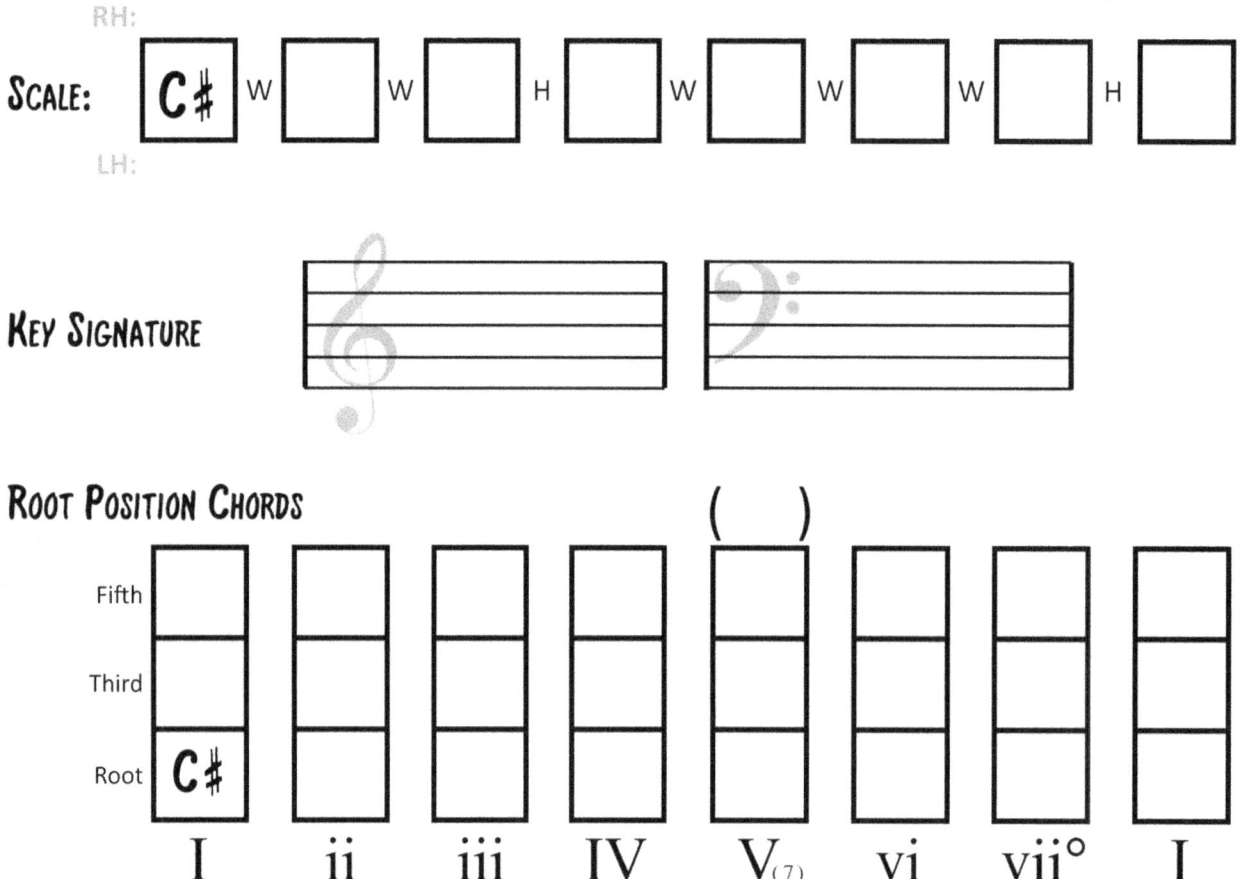

Suggested Practice for Root Position Chords:
1. Block the Chord using fingers 1, 3, and 5.
2. Name the chord.
3. Arpeggiate the chord (cross-hand arpeggios).

Cadence

Suggested Practice:
1. Play chords in the RH and play roots in the LH.
2. Try playing the cadence with different rhythms.
3. The cadence can be played as root position chords or by going chord to chord sharing common tones (inversions).

Major Scale written on the Staff

Root Position Chords Written on the Staff

Cadence Written on the Staff

C# MAJOR

BLUES SCALE:

(OPTIONAL)

RH:

☐ ☐ ☐ ☐ ☐ ☐ ☐ ☐
1 b3 4 b5 5 b7 1 b9

LH:

BLUES PROGRESSION:

ii V I

12-BAR BLUES PATTERN:

1) Four Measures of the I Chord.
2) Two Measures of the IV Chord.
3) Two Measures of the I Chord.
4) One Measure of the V Chord.
5) One Measure of the IV Chord.
6) Two Measures of the I Chord.

*You can try this with full chords or play just the root and fifth with your left hand while you improvise a melody from the blues scale with your right hand.

OCTAVE ARPEGGIOS SHARING TONIC

Major:
Write in the Root, 3rd, 5th, and octave of the Major Scale.

Augmented:
From Major, Raise 5th by a 1/2 step.

Minor:
From Major, Lower 3rd by a 1/2 step.

Diminished 7th:
From Major, Lower 3rd & 5th by a 1/2 step, and Lower 7th by a whole step.

Dominant 7th:
From Major, Lower 7th by a 1/2 step.

Blues Scale written on the Staff

Blues Progression written on the Staff

"Happy Birthday" in the key of C♯ (with Lead Sheet)

Parallel Minor Scales in C#

Natural:
From Major, lower the 3rd, 6th & 7th by a 1/2 step

RH:
| C# | W | | H | | W | | W | | W | | H | | W | | W | |

LH:

Natural Minor Scale written on the Staff

Key Signature

Harmonic:
From Natural Minor, raise the 7th back up a 1/2 step.

RH:
LH:

Melodic:
Ascending: From Major, lower the 3rd. Descending: Same as Natural Minor.

RH:
LH:

RH:
LH:

Explore: Composition in C♯

F MAJOR

Major Scale Pattern: W-W-H-W-W-W-H

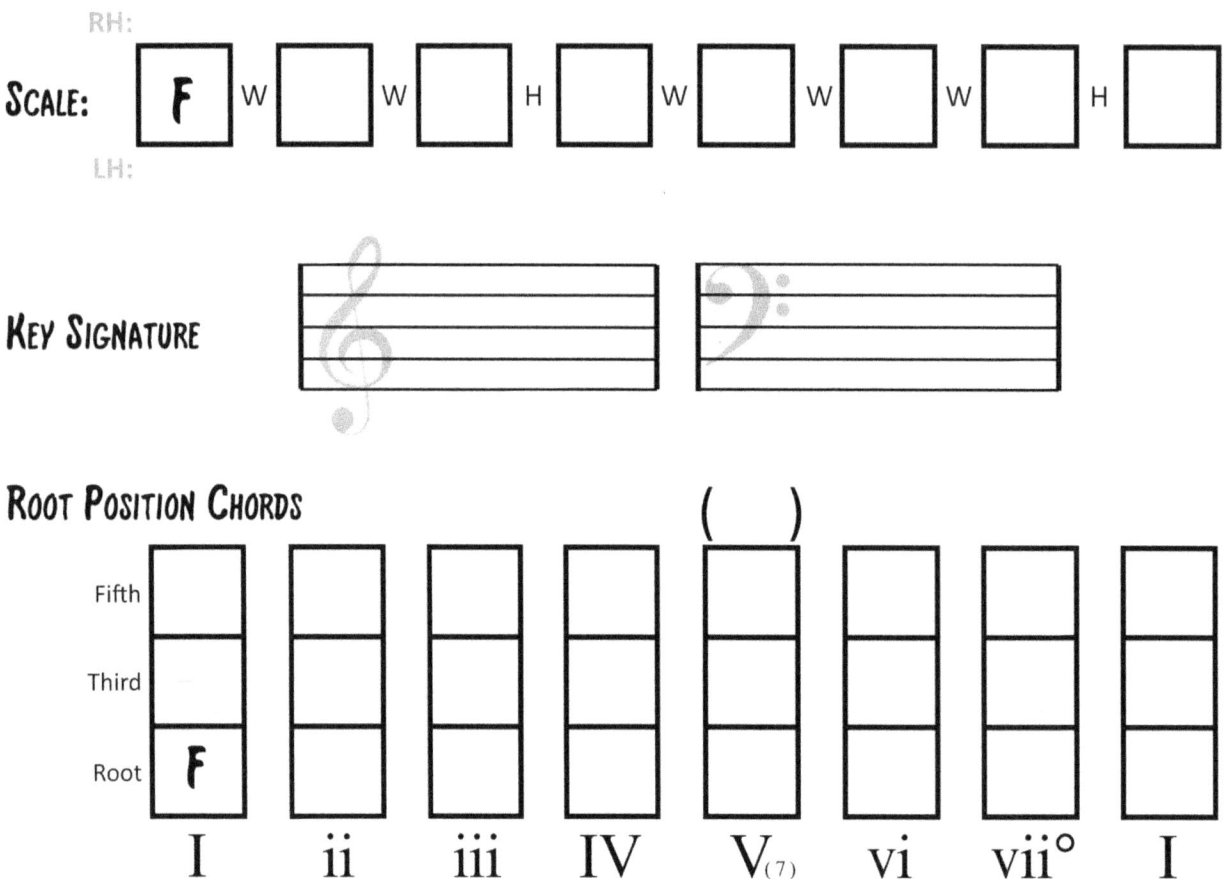

Suggested Practice for Root Position Chords:
1. Block the Chord using fingers 1, 3, and 5.
2. Name the chord.
3. Arpeggiate the chord (cross-hand arpeggios).

Cadence

Suggested Practice:
1. Play chords in the RH and play roots in the LH.
2. Try playing the cadence with different rhythms.
3. The cadence can be played as root position chords or by going chord to chord sharing common tones (inversions).

MAJOR SCALE WRITTEN ON THE STAFF

ROOT POSITION CHORDS WRITTEN ON THE STAFF

CADENCE WRITTEN ON THE STAFF

F MAJOR

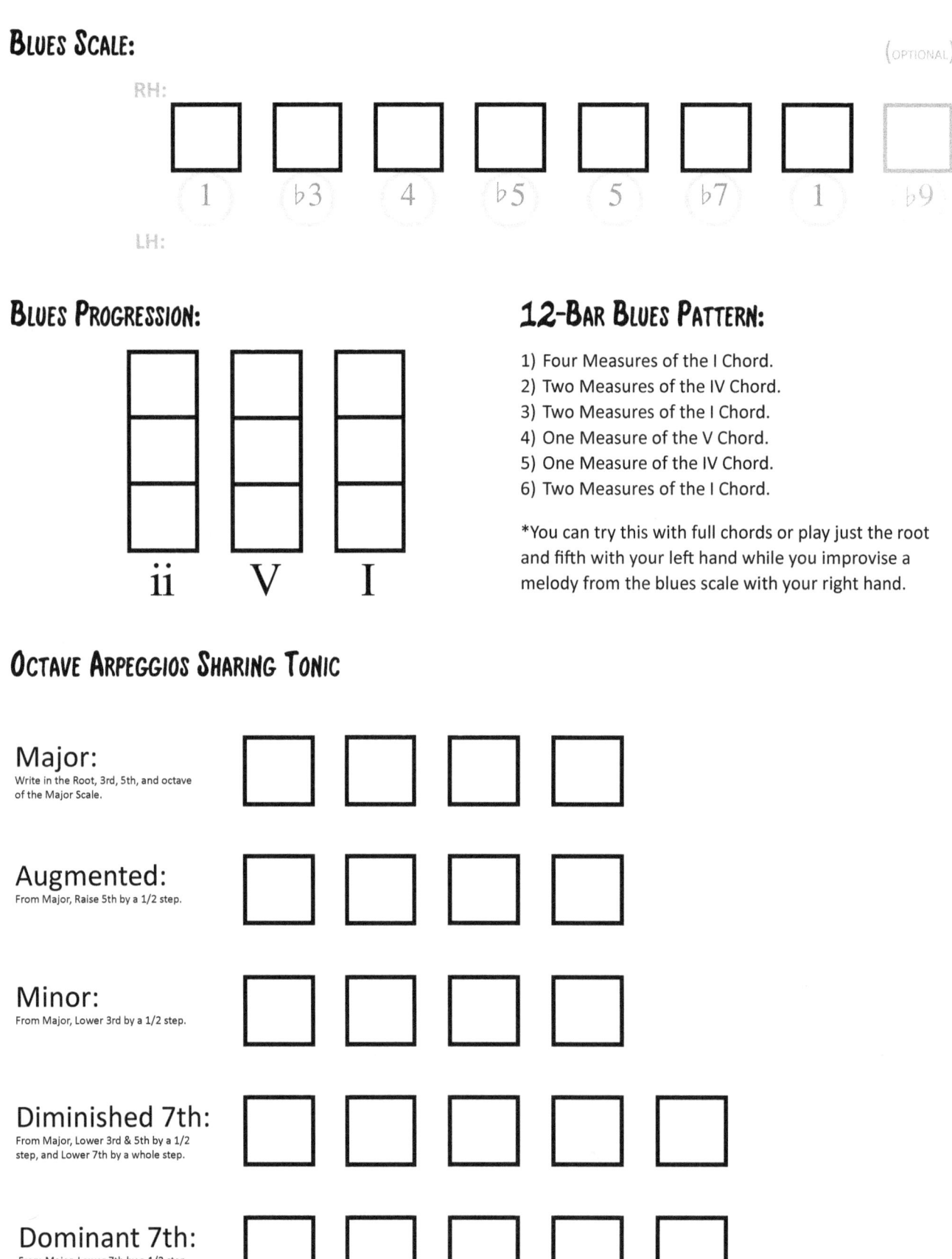

Blues Scale written on the Staff

Blues Progression written on the Staff

"Happy Birthday" in the Key of F (with Lead Sheet)

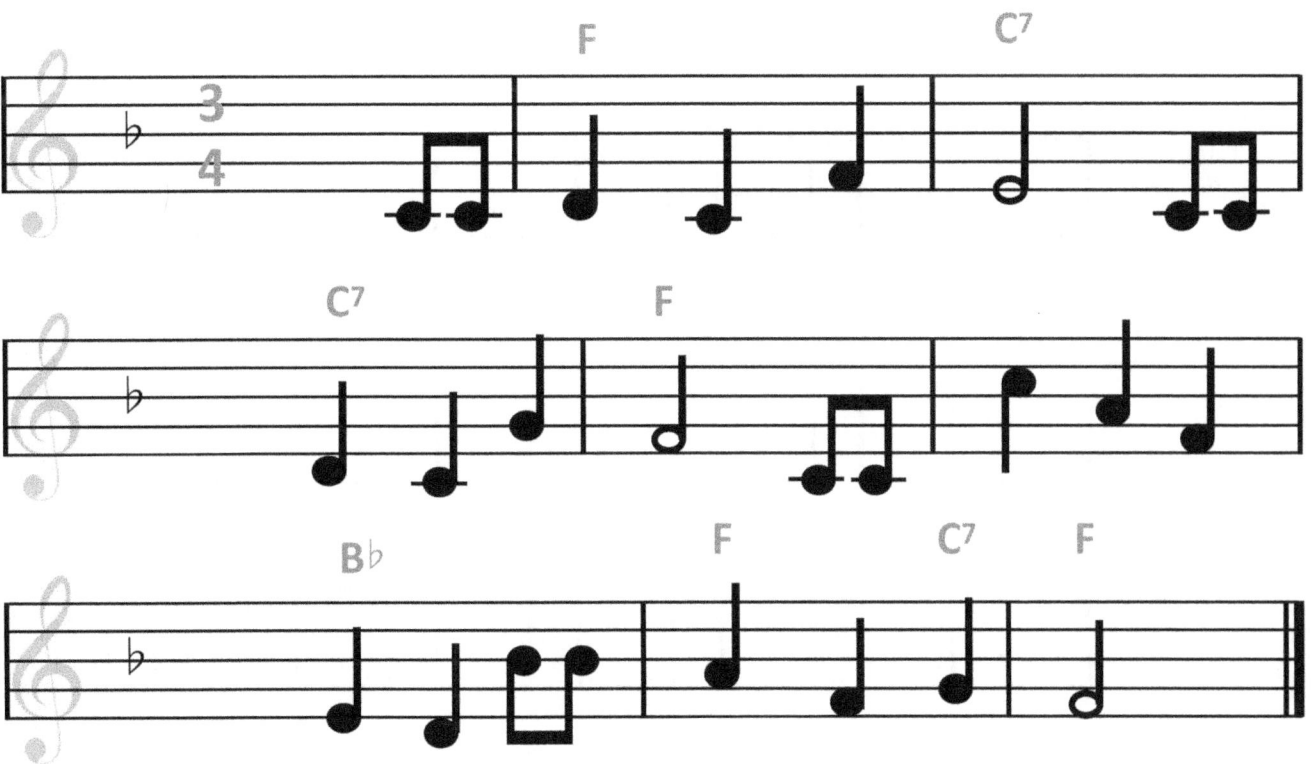

Parallel Minor Scales in F

Natural:
From Major, lower the 3rd, 6th & 7th by a 1/2 step

RH:

| F | W | | H | | W | | W | | H | | W | | W | |

LH:

Natural Minor Scale written on the Staff

Key Signature

Harmonic:
From Natural Minor, raise the 7th back up a 1/2 step.

RH:

LH:

Melodic:
Ascending: From Major, lower the 3rd. Descending: Same as Natural Minor.

RH:

LH:

RH:

LH:

Explore: Composition in F

B♭ Major

Major Scale Pattern: W-W-H-W-W-W-H

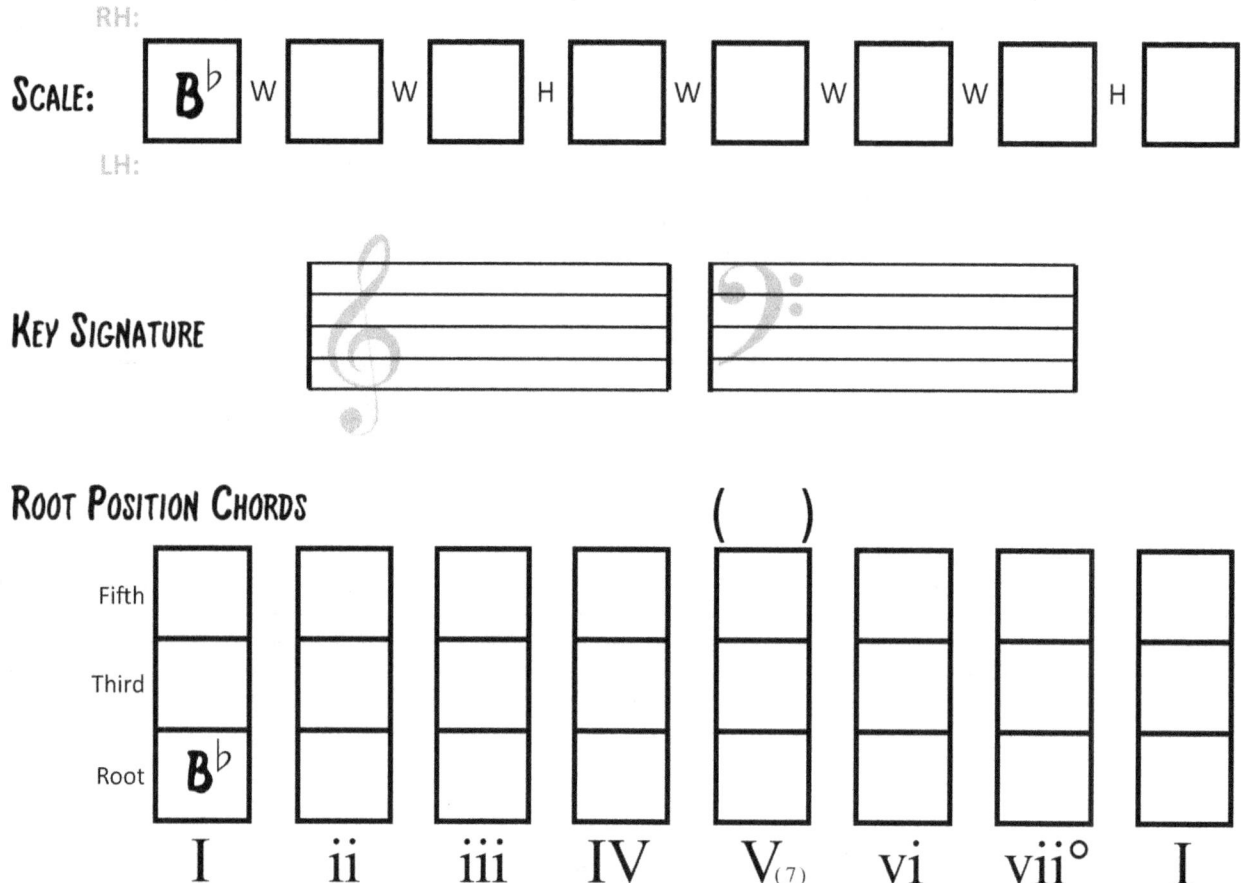

Suggested Practice for Root Position Chords:
1. Block the Chord using fingers 1, 3, and 5.
2. Name the chord.
3. Arpeggiate the chord (cross-hand arpeggios).

Cadence

Suggested Practice:
1. Play chords in the RH and play roots in the LH.
2. Try playing the cadence with different rhythms.
3. The cadence can be played as root position chords or by going chord to chord sharing common tones (inversions).

MAJOR SCALE WRITTEN ON THE STAFF

ROOT POSITION CHORDS WRITTEN ON THE STAFF

CADENCE WRITTEN ON THE STAFF

B♭ MAJOR

BLUES SCALE:

RH:

☐ ☐ ☐ ☐ ☐ ☐ ☐ ☐ (OPTIONAL)

1   ♭3   4   ♭5   5   ♭7   1   ♭9

LH:

BLUES PROGRESSION:

ii   V   I

12-BAR BLUES PATTERN:

1) Four Measures of the I Chord.
2) Two Measures of the IV Chord.
3) Two Measures of the I Chord.
4) One Measure of the V Chord.
5) One Measure of the IV Chord.
6) Two Measures of the I Chord.

*You can try this with full chords or play just the root and fifth with your left hand while you improvise a melody from the blues scale with your right hand.

OCTAVE ARPEGGIOS SHARING TONIC

Major:
Write in the Root, 3rd, 5th, and octave of the Major Scale.

Augmented:
From Major, Raise 5th by a 1/2 step.

Minor:
From Major, Lower 3rd by a 1/2 step.

Diminished 7th:
From Major, Lower 3rd & 5th by a 1/2 step, and Lower 7th by a whole step.

Dominant 7th:
From Major, Lower 7th by a 1/2 step.

Blues Scale written on the Staff

Blues Progression written on the Staff

"Happy Birthday" in the key of B♭ (with Lead Sheet)

Parallel Minor Scales in B♭

Natural:
From Major, lower the 3rd, 6th & 7th by a 1/2 step

RH:
| B♭ | W | | H | | W | | W | | H | | W | | W | |

LH:

Natural Minor Scale written on the Staff

Key Signature

Harmonic:
From Natural Minor, raise the 7th back up a 1/2 step.

RH:
LH:

Melodic:
Ascending: From Major, lower the 3rd. Descending: Same as Natural Minor.

RH:
LH:

RH:
LH:

Explore: Composition in B♭

E♭ Major

Major Scale Pattern: W-W-H-W-W-W-H

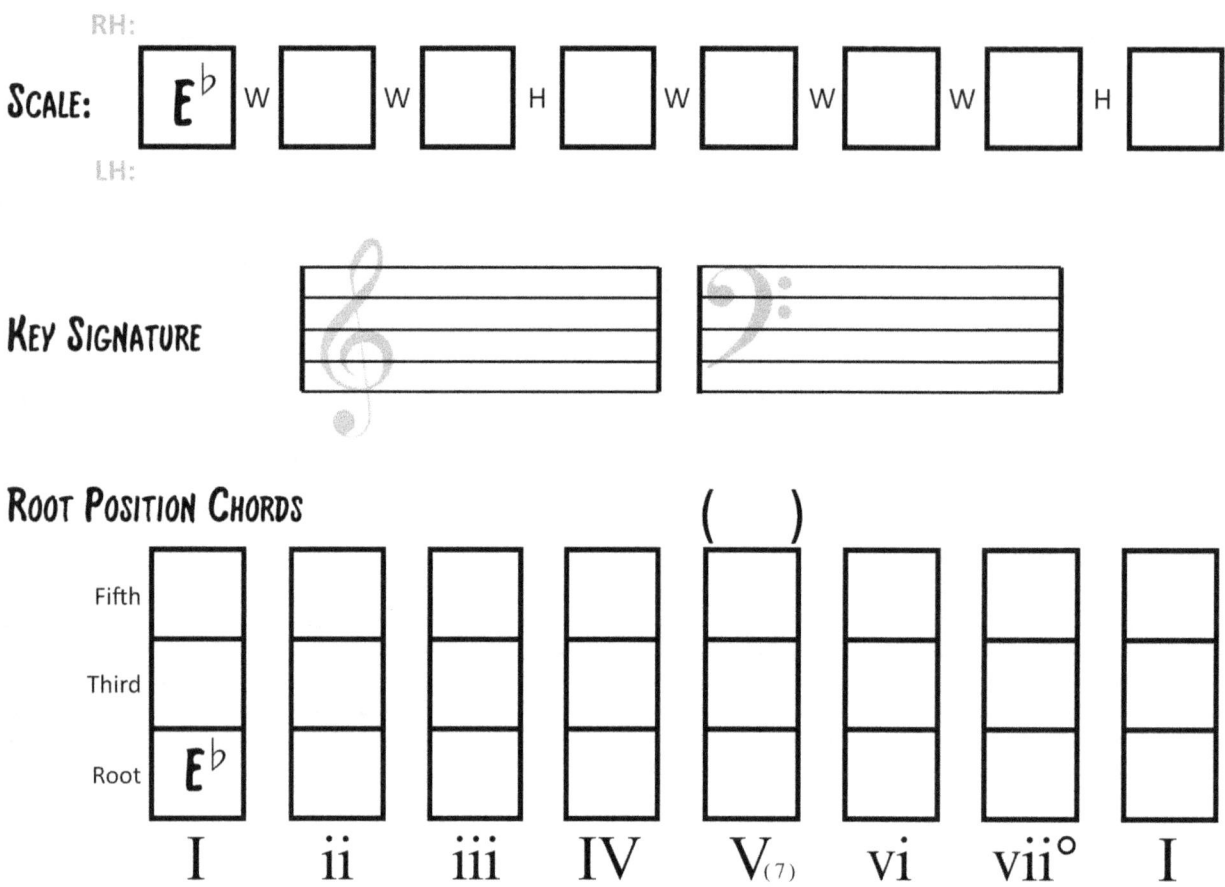

Suggested Practice for Root Position Chords:
1. Block the Chord using fingers 1, 3, and 5.
2. Name the chord.
3. Arpeggiate the chord (cross-hand arpeggios).

Cadence

Suggested Practice:
1. Play chords in the RH and play roots in the LH.
2. Try playing the cadence with different rhythms.
3. The cadence can be played as root position chords or by going chord to chord sharing common tones (inversions).

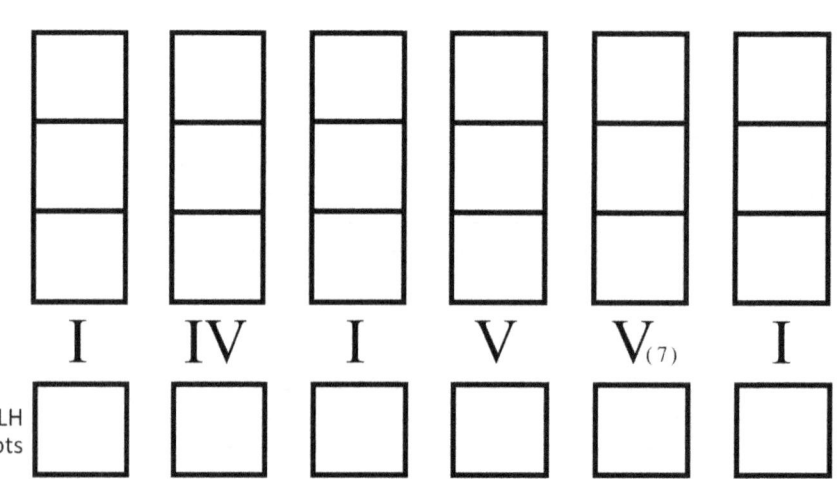

Major Scale written on the Staff

Root Position Chords Written on the Staff

Cadence Written on the Staff

E♭ MAJOR

BLUES SCALE:

RH:

☐ ☐ ☐ ☐ ☐ ☐ ☐ ☐ (OPTIONAL)

1　♭3　4　♭5　5　♭7　1　♭9

LH:

BLUES PROGRESSION:

ii　V　I

12-BAR BLUES PATTERN:

1) Four Measures of the I Chord.
2) Two Measures of the IV Chord.
3) Two Measures of the I Chord.
4) One Measure of the V Chord.
5) One Measure of the IV Chord.
6) Two Measures of the I Chord.

*You can try this with full chords or play just the root and fifth with your left hand while you improvise a melody from the blues scale with your right hand.

OCTAVE ARPEGGIOS SHARING TONIC

Major:
Write in the Root, 3rd, 5th, and octave of the Major Scale.

Augmented:
From Major, Raise 5th by a 1/2 step.

Minor:
From Major, Lower 3rd by a 1/2 step.

Diminished 7th:
From Major, Lower 3rd & 5th by a 1/2 step, and Lower 7th by a whole step.

Dominant 7th:
From Major, Lower 7th by a 1/2 step.

Blues Scale written on the Staff

Blues Progression written on the Staff

"Happy Birthday" in the Key of E♭ (with Lead Sheet)

75

Parallel Minor Scales in E♭

Natural:
From Major, lower the 3rd, 6th & 7th by a 1/2 step

RH:
| E♭ | W | | H | | W | | W | | H | | W | | W | |

LH:

Natural Minor Scale written on the Staff

Key Signature

Harmonic:
From Natural Minor, raise the 7th back up a 1/2 step.

RH:
LH:

Melodic:
Ascending: From Major, lower the 3rd. Descending: Same as Natural Minor.

RH:
LH:

RH:
LH:

Explore: Composition in E♭

A♭ MAJOR

Major Scale Pattern: W-W-H-W-W-W-H

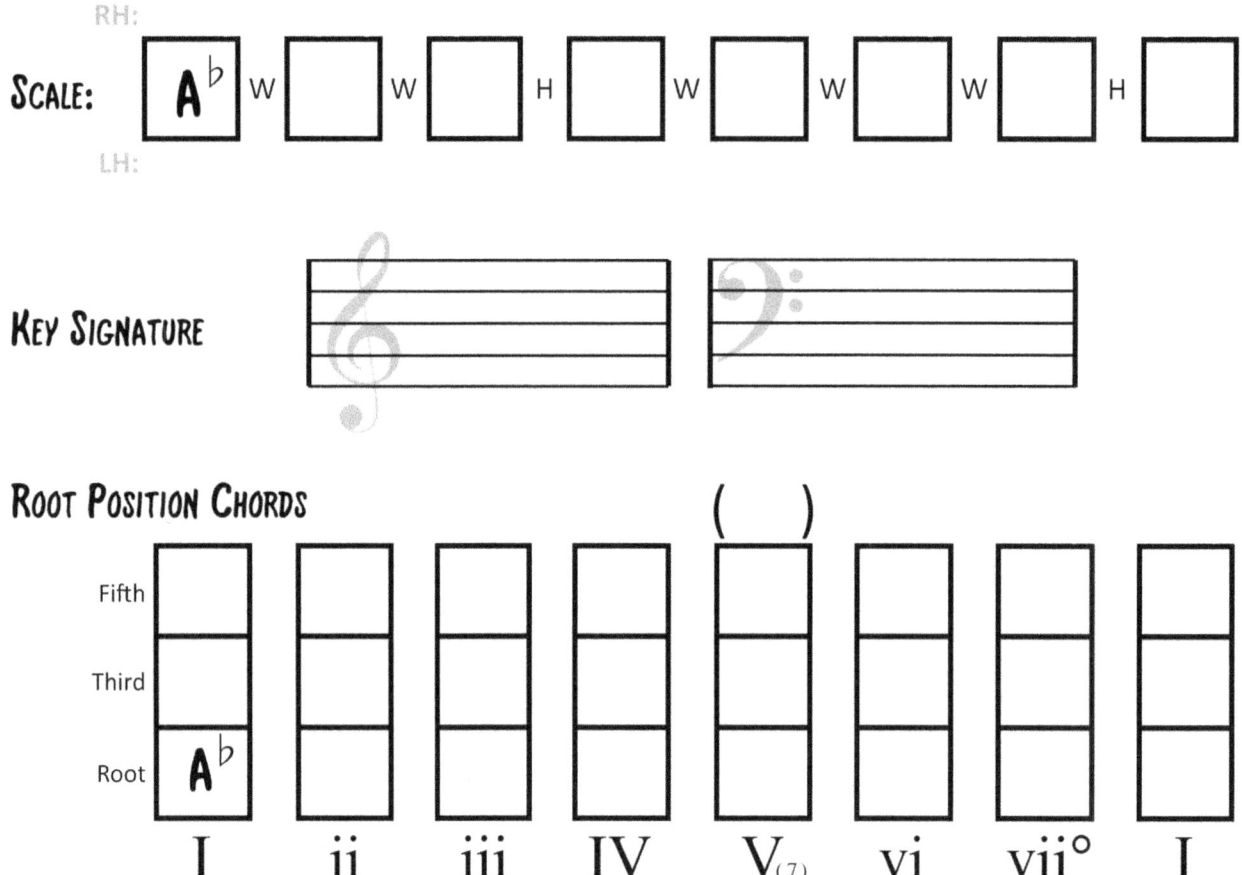

Suggested Practice for Root Position Chords:
1. Block the Chord using fingers 1, 3, and 5.
2. Name the chord.
3. Arpeggiate the chord (cross-hand arpeggios).

CADENCE

Suggested Practice:
1. Play chords in the RH and play roots in the LH.
2. Try playing the cadence with different rhythms.
3. The cadence can be played as root position chords or by going chord to chord sharing common tones (inversions).

Major Scale Written on the Staff

Root Position Chords Written on the Staff

Cadence Written on the Staff

A♭ MAJOR

BLUES SCALE:

(OPTIONAL)

RH:

☐ ☐ ☐ ☐ ☐ ☐ ☐ ☐

1 ♭3 4 ♭5 5 ♭7 1 ♭9

LH:

BLUES PROGRESSION:

ii V I

12-BAR BLUES PATTERN:

1) Four Measures of the I Chord.
2) Two Measures of the IV Chord.
3) Two Measures of the I Chord.
4) One Measure of the V Chord.
5) One Measure of the IV Chord.
6) Two Measures of the I Chord.

*You can try this with full chords or play just the root and fifth with your left hand while you improvise a melody from the blues scale with your right hand.

OCTAVE ARPEGGIOS SHARING TONIC

Major:
Write in the Root, 3rd, 5th, and octave of the Major Scale.

☐ ☐ ☐ ☐

Augmented:
From Major, Raise 5th by a 1/2 step.

☐ ☐ ☐ ☐

Minor:
From Major, Lower 3rd by a 1/2 step.

☐ ☐ ☐ ☐

Diminished 7th:
From Major, Lower 3rd & 5th by a 1/2 step, and Lower 7th by a whole step.

☐ ☐ ☐ ☐ ☐

Dominant 7th:
From Major, Lower 7th by a 1/2 step.

☐ ☐ ☐ ☐ ☐

Blues Scale written on the Staff

Blues Progression written on the Staff

"Happy Birthday" in the key of A♭ (with Lead Sheet)

Parallel Minor Scales in A♭

Natural:
From Major, lower the 3rd, 6th & 7th by a 1/2 step

RH: | A♭ | W | | H | W | W | H | W | W |
LH:

Natural Minor Scale written on the Staff

Key Signature

Harmonic:
From Natural Minor, raise the 7th back up a 1/2 step.

RH:
LH:

Melodic:
Ascending: From Major, lower the 3rd. Descending: Same as Natural Minor.

RH:
LH:

RH:
LH:

82

Explore: Composition in A♭

D♭ MAJOR

Major Scale Pattern: W-W-H-W-W-W-H

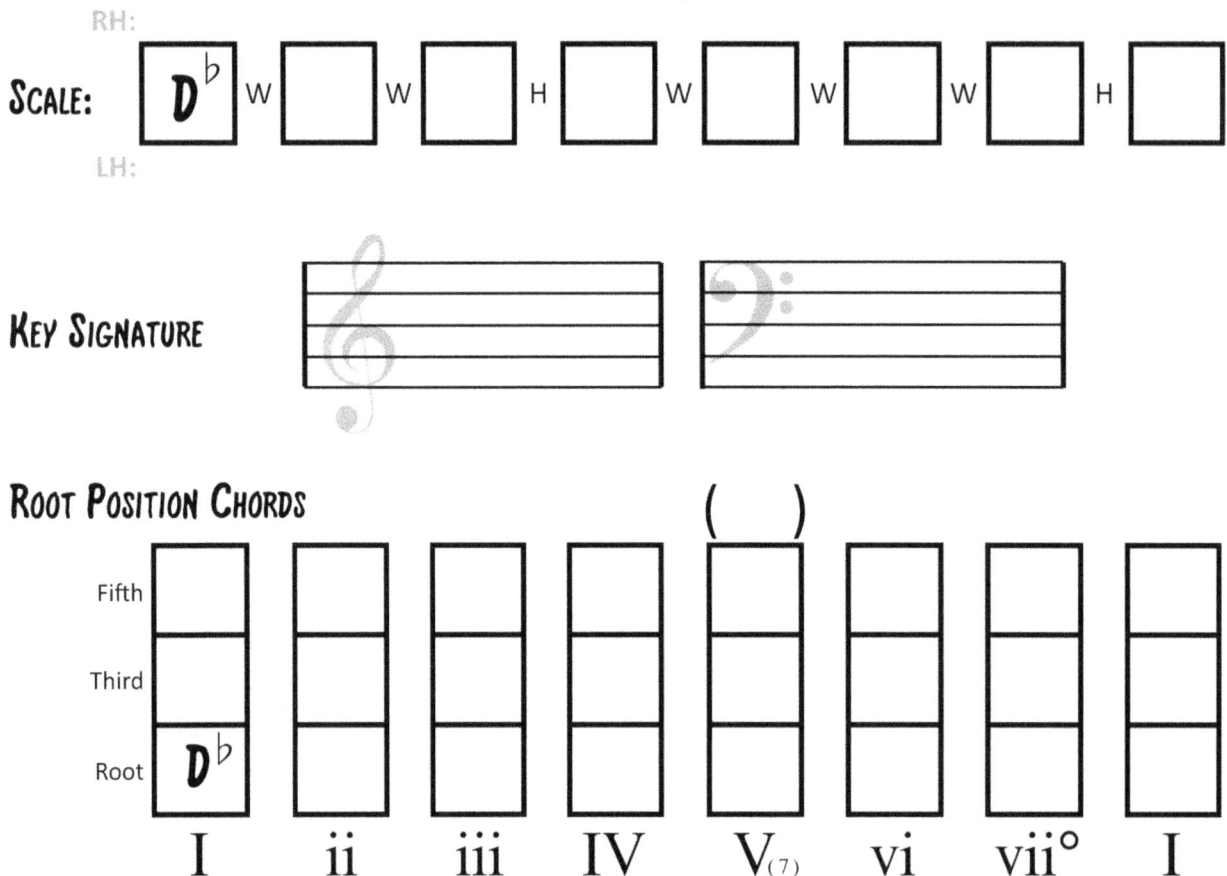

Suggested Practice for Root Position Chords:
1. Block the Chord using fingers 1, 3, and 5.
2. Name the chord.
3. Arpeggiate the chord (cross-hand arpeggios).

CADENCE

Suggested Practice:
1. Play chords in the RH and play roots in the LH.
2. Try playing the cadence with different rhythms.
3. The cadence can be played as root position chords or by going chord to chord sharing common tones (inversions).

Major Scale Written on the Staff

Root Position Chords Written on the Staff

Cadence Written on the Staff

D♭ Major

Blues Scale:
(OPTIONAL)

RH:
☐ ☐ ☐ ☐ ☐ ☐ ☐ ☐
1 ♭3 4 ♭5 5 ♭7 1 ♭9

LH:

Blues Progression:

☐☐☐
☐☐☐
☐☐☐
ii V I

12-Bar Blues Pattern:

1) Four Measures of the I Chord.
2) Two Measures of the IV Chord.
3) Two Measures of the I Chord.
4) One Measure of the V Chord.
5) One Measure of the IV Chord.
6) Two Measures of the I Chord.

*You can try this with full chords or play just the root and fifth with your left hand while you improvise a melody from the blues scale with your right hand.

Octave Arpeggios Sharing Tonic

Major:
Write in the Root, 3rd, 5th, and octave of the Major Scale.
☐ ☐ ☐ ☐

Augmented:
From Major, Raise 5th by a 1/2 step.
☐ ☐ ☐ ☐

Minor:
From Major, Lower 3rd by a 1/2 step.
☐ ☐ ☐ ☐

Diminished 7th:
From Major, Lower 3rd & 5th by a 1/2 step, and Lower 7th by a whole step.
☐ ☐ ☐ ☐ ☐

Dominant 7th:
From Major, Lower 7th by a 1/2 step.
☐ ☐ ☐ ☐ ☐

Blues Scale written on the Staff

Blues Progression written on the Staff

"Happy Birthday" in the key of D♭ (with Lead Sheet)

Parallel Minor Scales in D♭

Natural:
From Major, lower the 3rd, 6th & 7th by a 1/2 step

RH:
| D♭ | W | | H | | W | | W | | W | | H | | W | | W | |

LH:

Natural Minor Scale written on the Staff

Key Signature

Harmonic:
From Natural Minor, raise the 7th back up a 1/2 step.

RH:
LH:

Melodic:
Ascending: From Major, lower the 3rd. Descending: Same as Natural Minor.

RH:
LH:

RH:
LH:

88

Explore: Composition in D♭

G♭ MAJOR

Major Scale Pattern: W-W-H-W-W-W-H

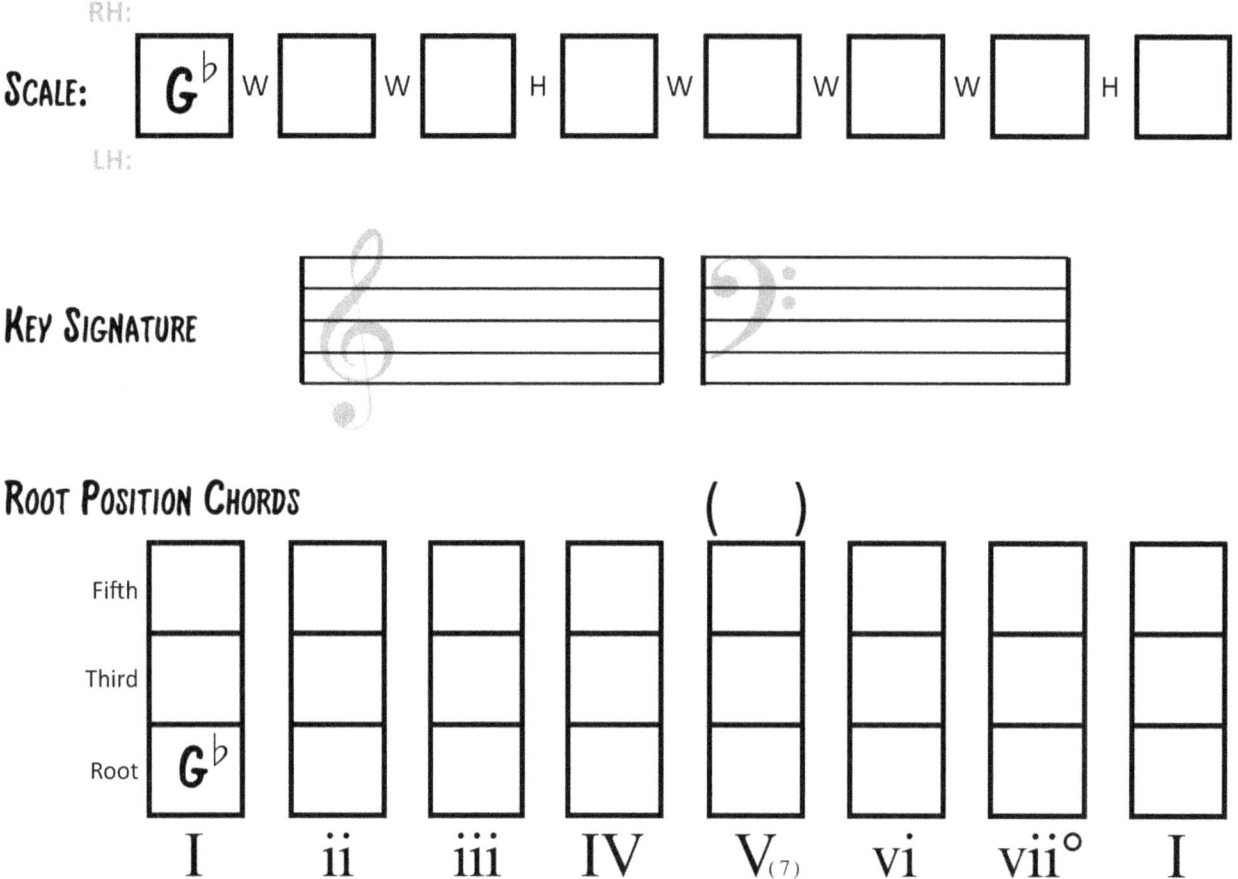

Suggested Practice for Root Position Chords:
1. Block the Chord using fingers 1, 3, and 5.
2. Name the chord.
3. Arpeggiate the chord (cross-hand arpeggios).

Cadence

Suggested Practice:
1. Play chords in the RH and play roots in the LH.
2. Try playing the cadence with different rhythms.
3. The cadence can be played as root position chords or by going chord to chord sharing common tones (inversions).

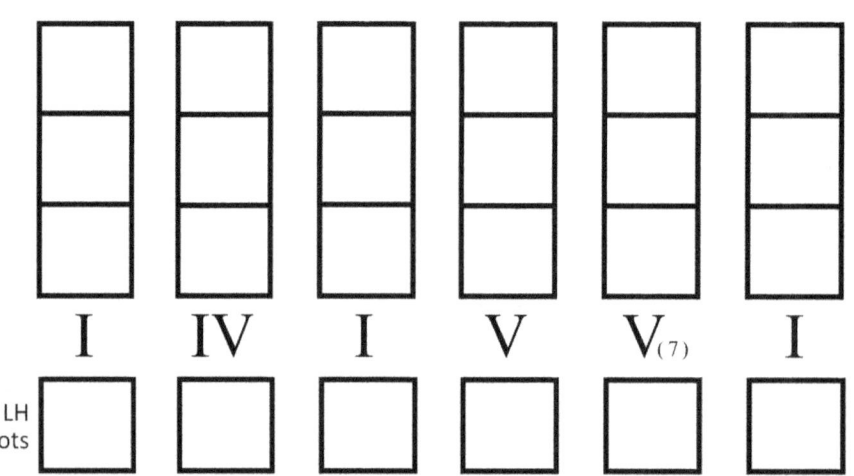

Major Scale written on the Staff

Root Position Chords Written on the Staff

Cadence Written on the Staff

G♭ Major

Blues Scale:

(Optional)

RH:

1 ♭3 4 ♭5 5 ♭7 1 ♭9

LH:

Blues Progression:

ii V I

12-Bar Blues Pattern:

1) Four Measures of the I Chord.
2) Two Measures of the IV Chord.
3) Two Measures of the I Chord.
4) One Measure of the V Chord.
5) One Measure of the IV Chord.
6) Two Measures of the I Chord.

*You can try this with full chords or play just the root and fifth with your left hand while you improvise a melody from the blues scale with your right hand.

Octave Arpeggios Sharing Tonic

Major:
Write in the Root, 3rd, 5th, and octave of the Major Scale.

Augmented:
From Major, Raise 5th by a 1/2 step.

Minor:
From Major, Lower 3rd by a 1/2 step.

Diminished 7th:
From Major, Lower 3rd & 5th by a 1/2 step, and Lower 7th by a whole step.

Dominant 7th:
From Major, Lower 7th by a 1/2 step.

Blues Scale written on the Staff

Blues Progression written on the Staff

"Happy Birthday" in the key of G♭ (with Lead Sheet)

93

Parallel Minor Scales in G♭

Natural:
From Major, lower the 3rd, 6th & 7th by a 1/2 step

RH:
| G♭ | W | | H | | W | | W | | H | | W | | W | |

LH:

Natural Minor Scale written on the Staff

Key Signature

Harmonic:
From Natural Minor, raise the 7th back up a 1/2 step.

RH:
LH:

Melodic:
Ascending: From Major, lower the 3rd. Descending: Same as Natural Minor.

RH:
LH:

RH:
LH:

Explore: Composition in G♭

Relative Minor Scales

Relative minor scales share the same key signature as their "relative" major key. This minor scale is also built on the sixth scale degree of its corresponding major scale. For example, a-minor is the relative minor to C major. In the exercises below, write the name of the correct minor scales next to the proper relative major scales.

MAJOR SCALES	RELATIVE MINOR SCALES
C Major	_____
G Major	_____
D Major	_____
A Major	_____
E Major	_____
B Major	_____
F # Major	_____
C # Major	_____
F Major	_____
B ♭ Major	_____
E ♭ Major	_____
A ♭ Major	_____
D ♭ Major	_____
G ♭ Major	_____
C ♭ Major	_____
F ♭ Major	_____

INVERSIONS

A chord inversion occurs when the order of notes is rearranged. However, the spelling of the chord remains unchanged. Take a look at the examples below using a C Major Chord.

The first chord is in **root position**, meaning that the root of the chord in the bass (the lowest note played). In the second chord, the third of the chord is now in the bass. We refer to this as **first inversion**. In the third example, the fifth of the chord is in the bass, which is referred to as **second inversion**.

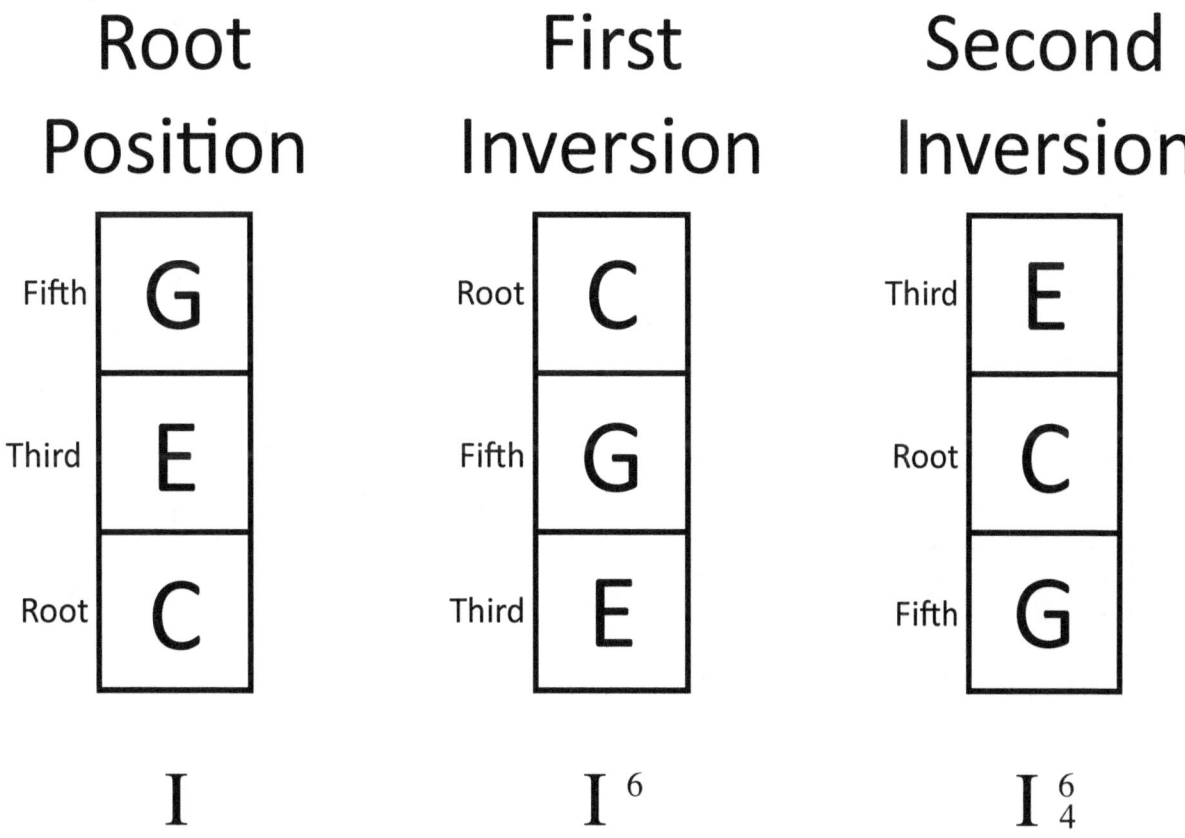

C MAJOR

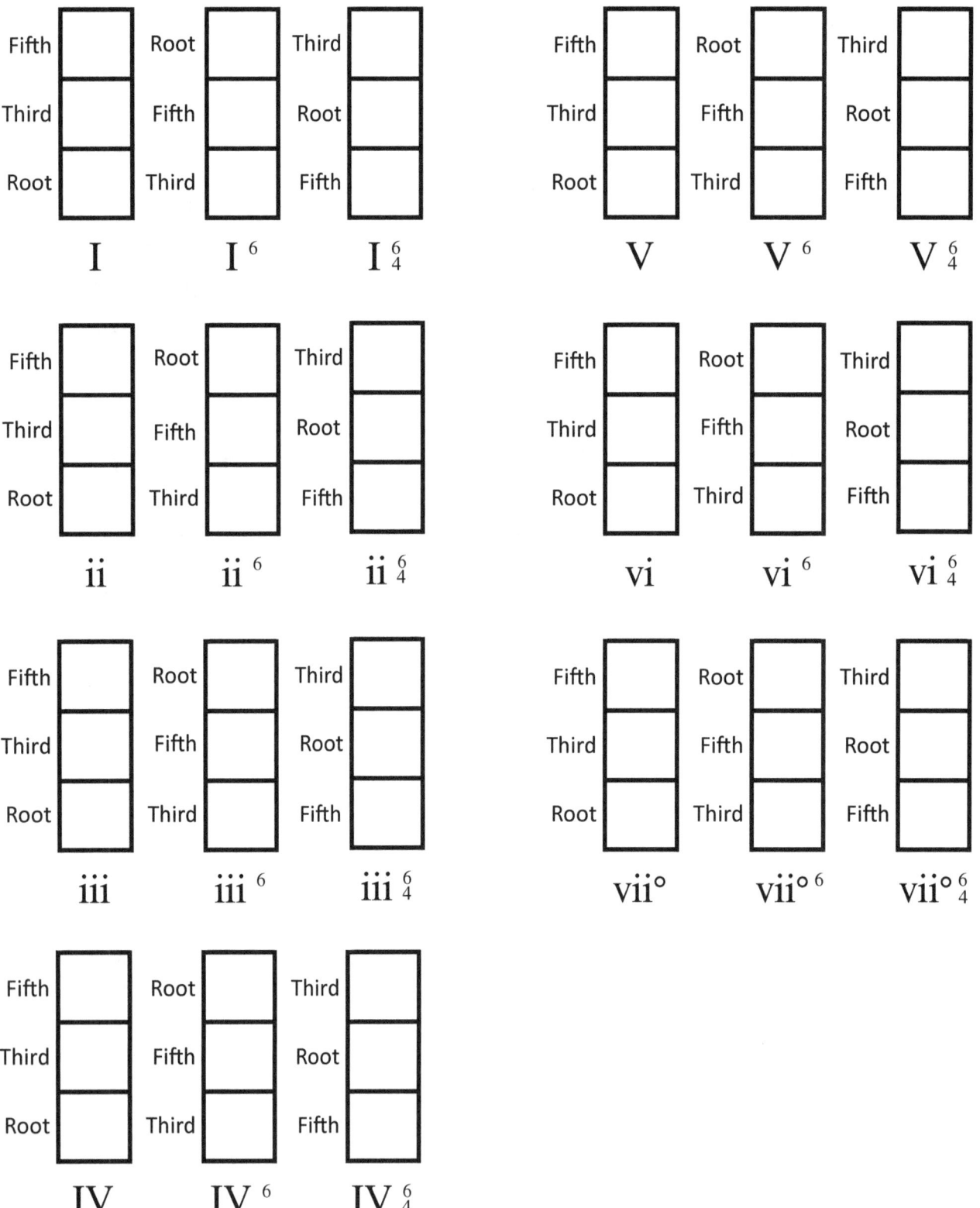

G MAJOR

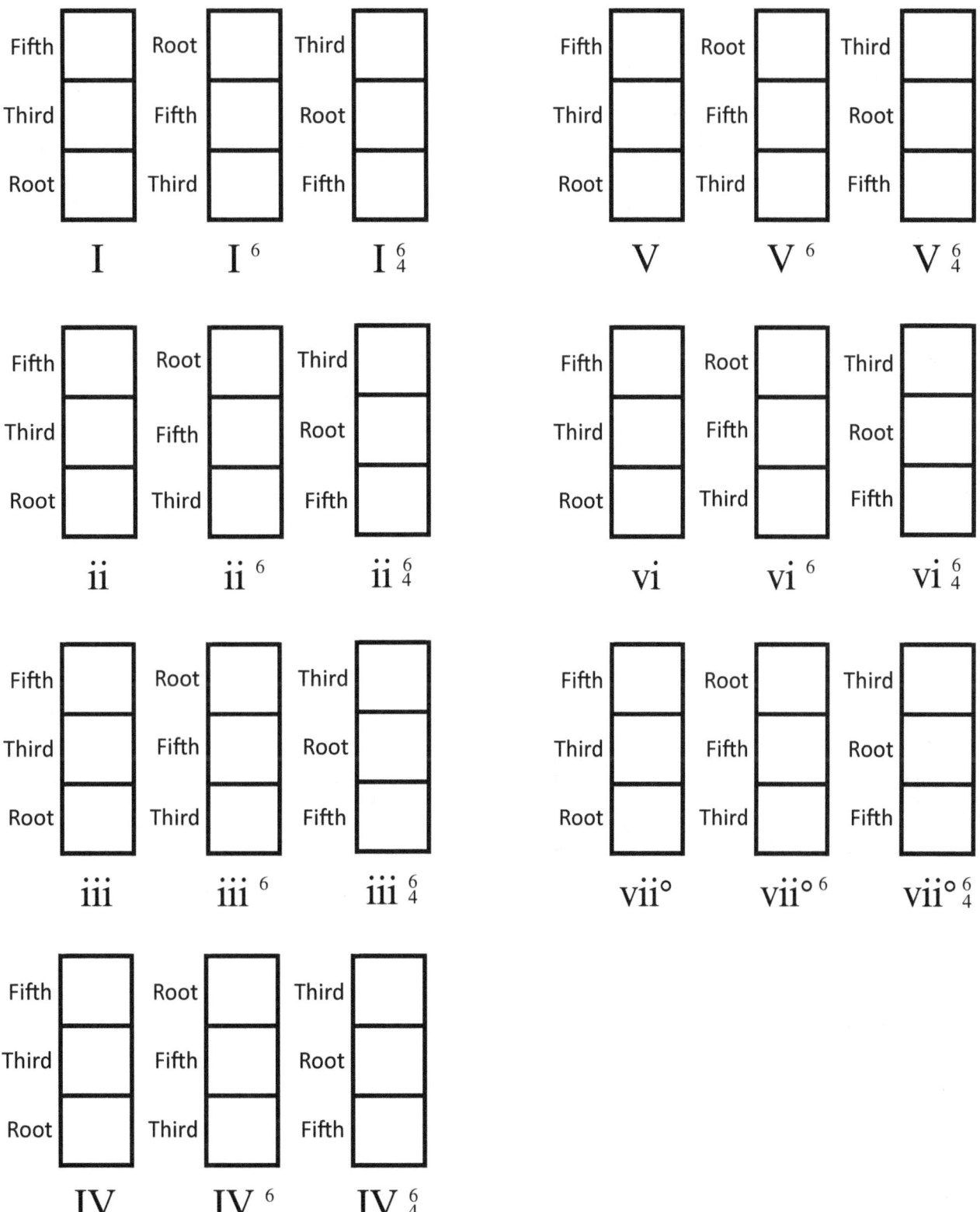

D MAJOR

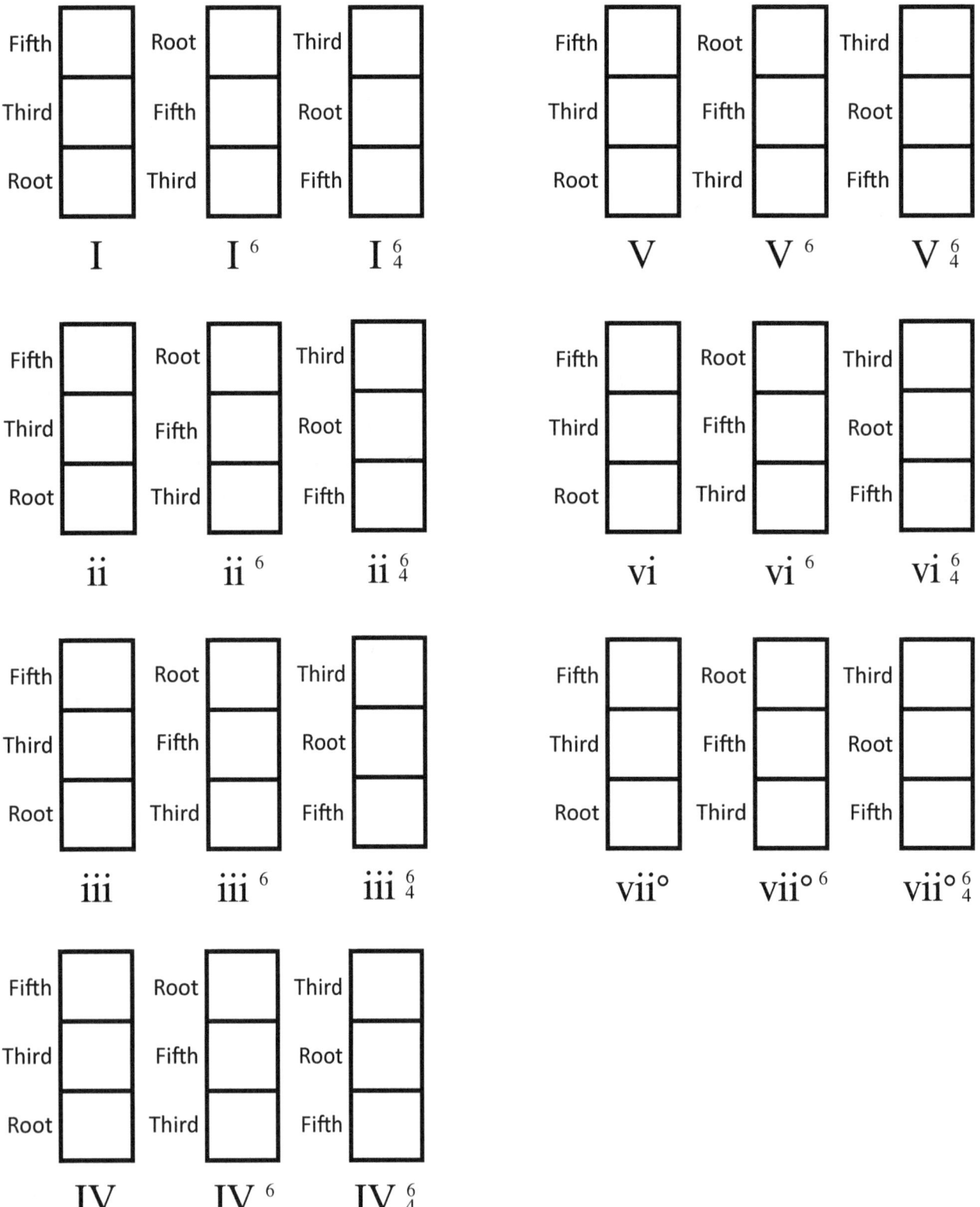

A MAJOR

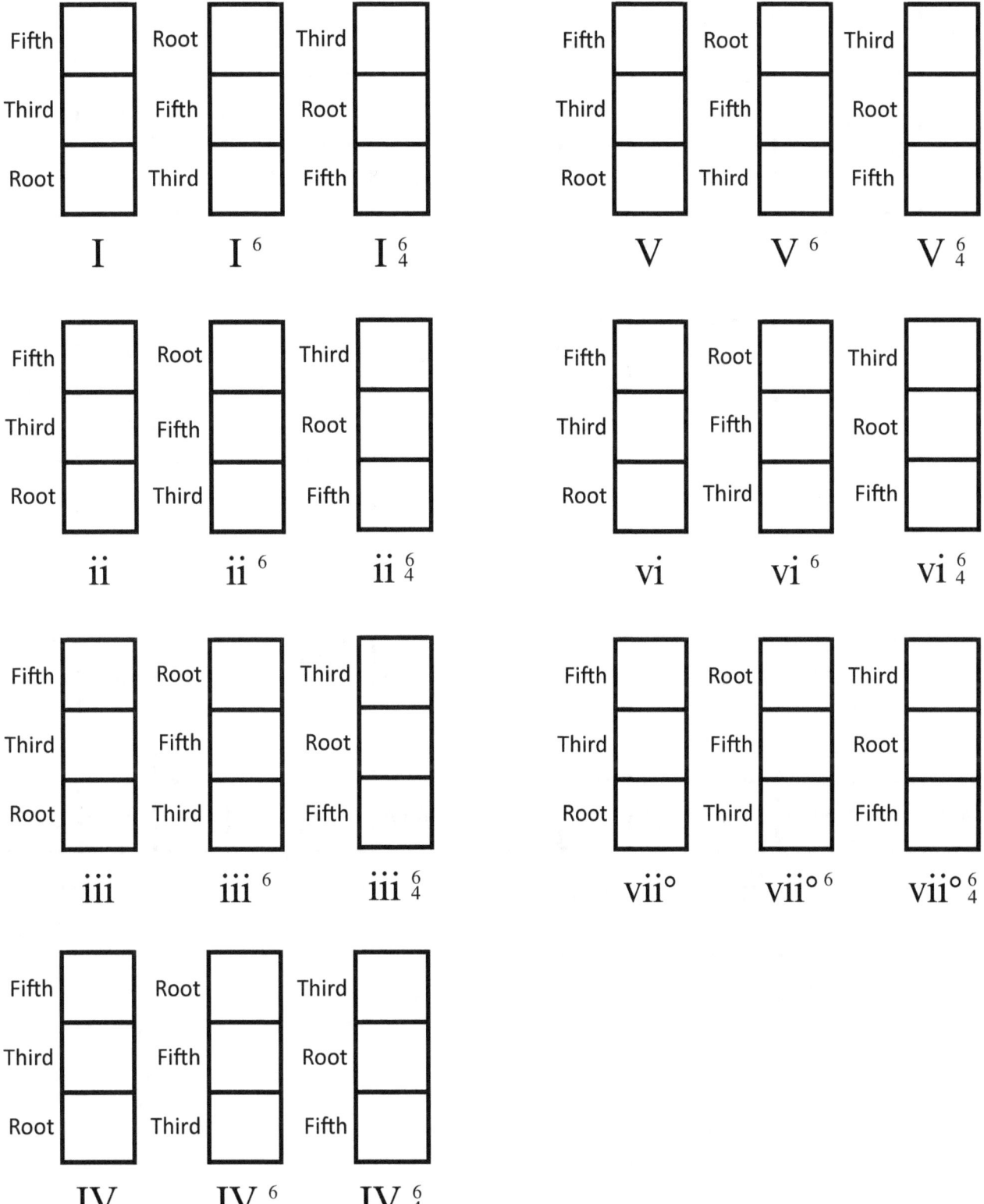

E MAJOR

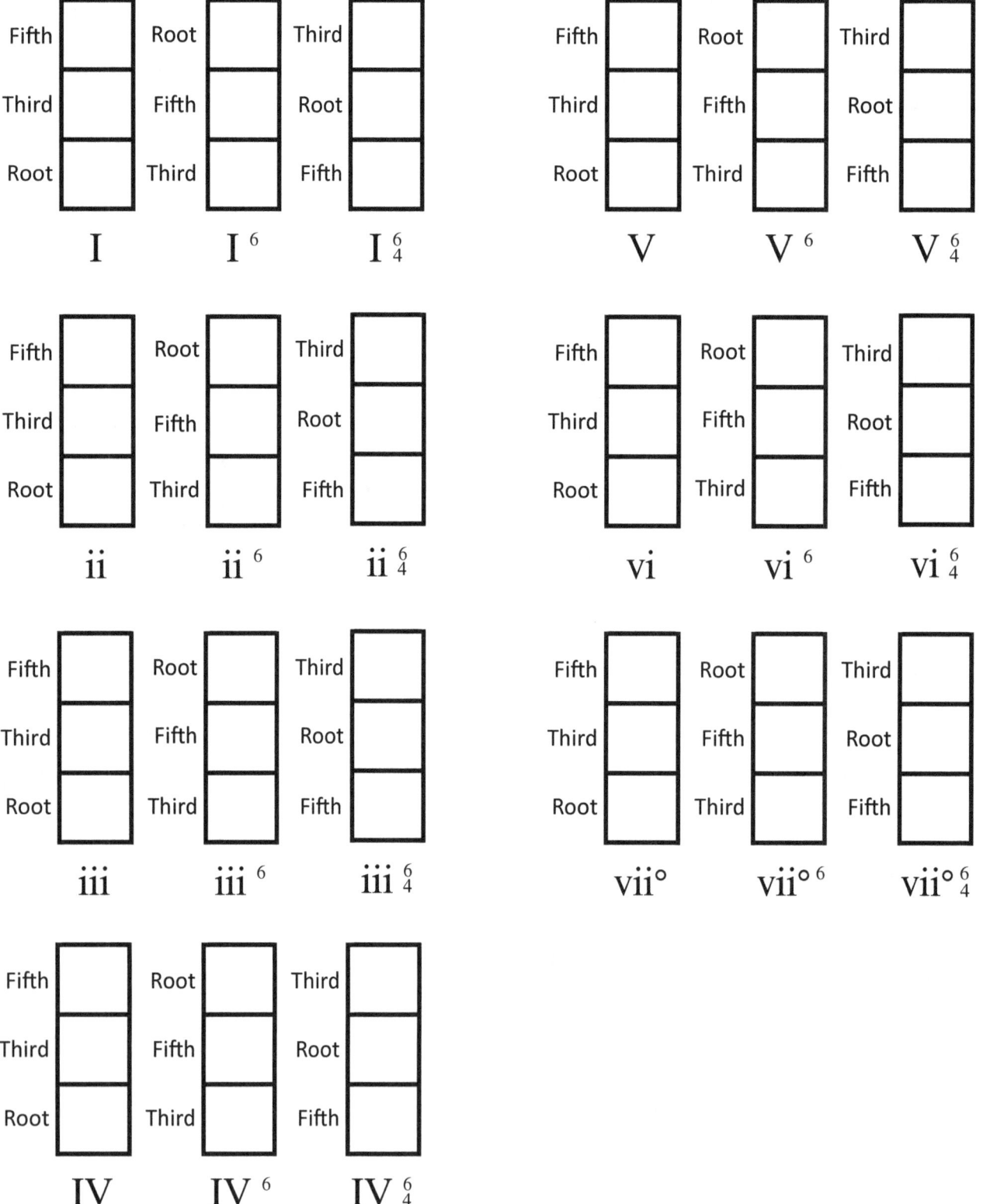

B MAJOR

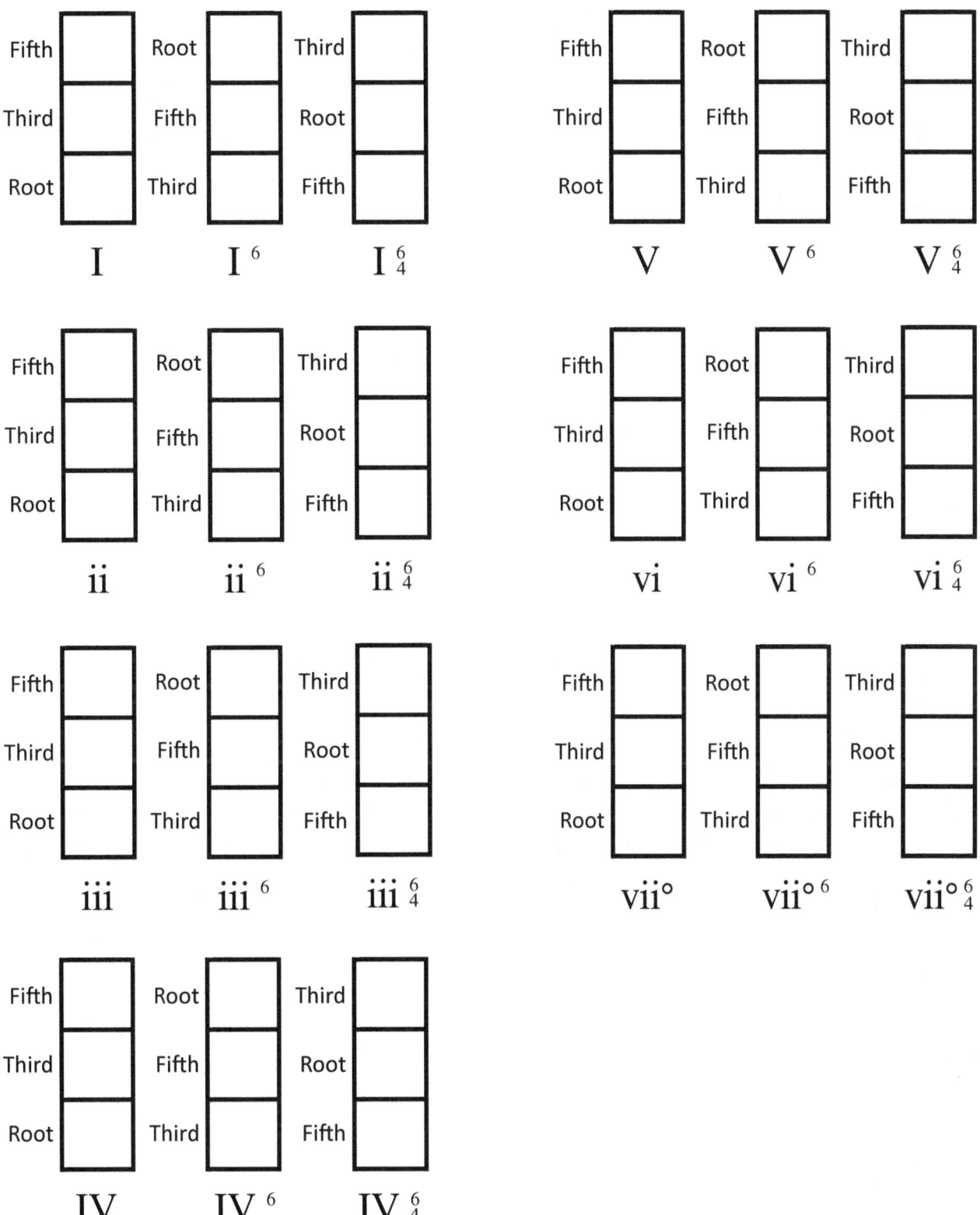

F# MAJOR

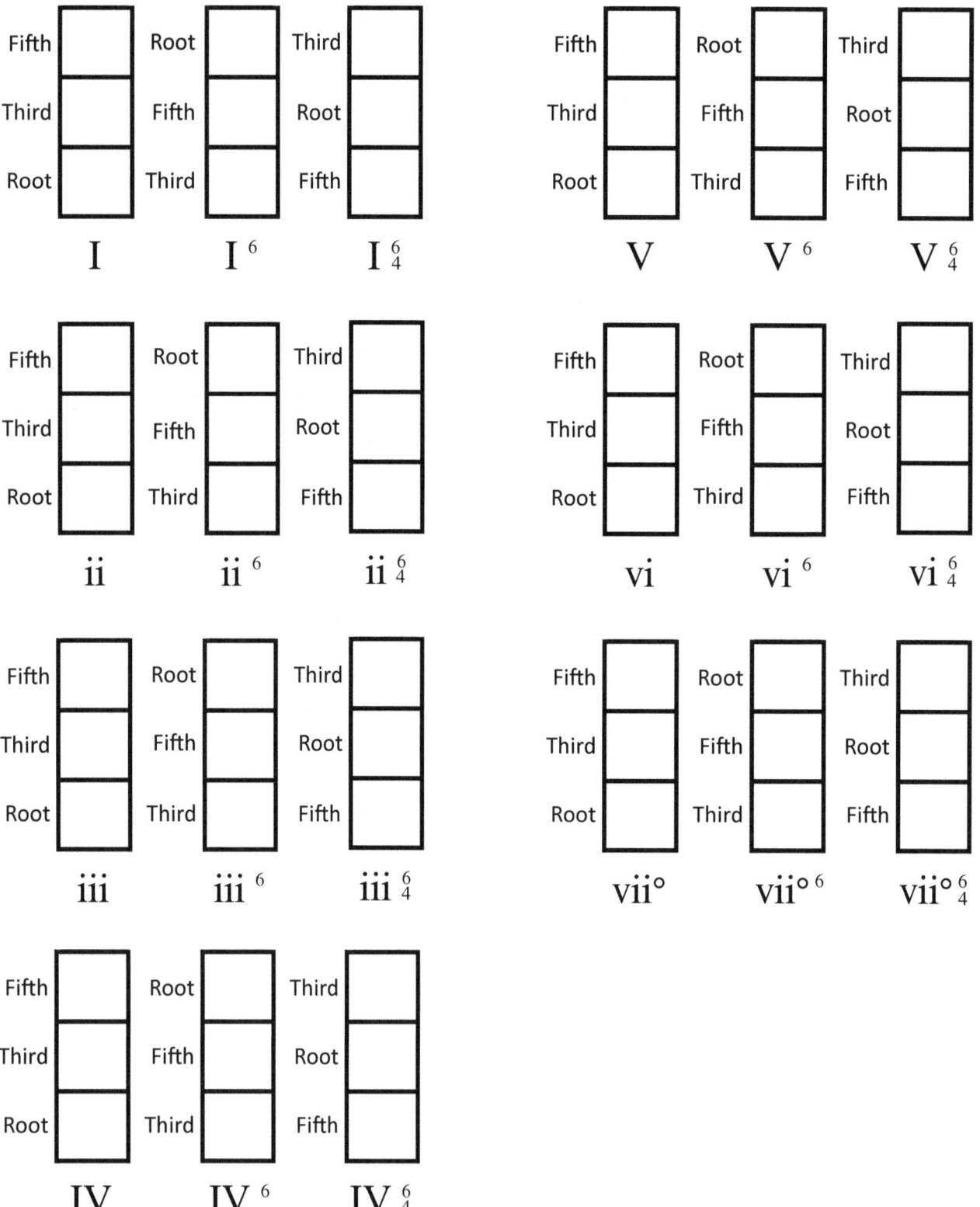

C# MAJOR

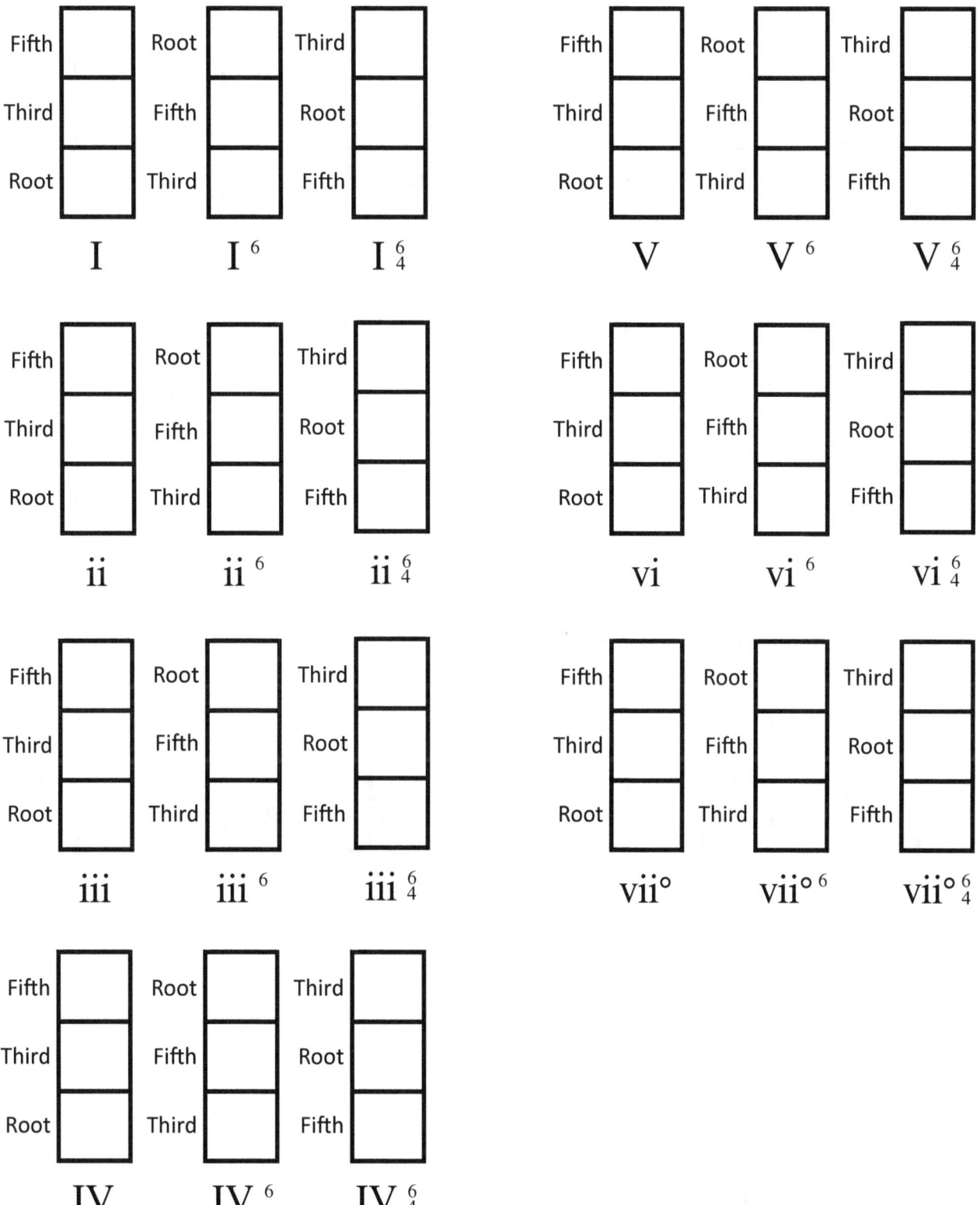

F MAJOR

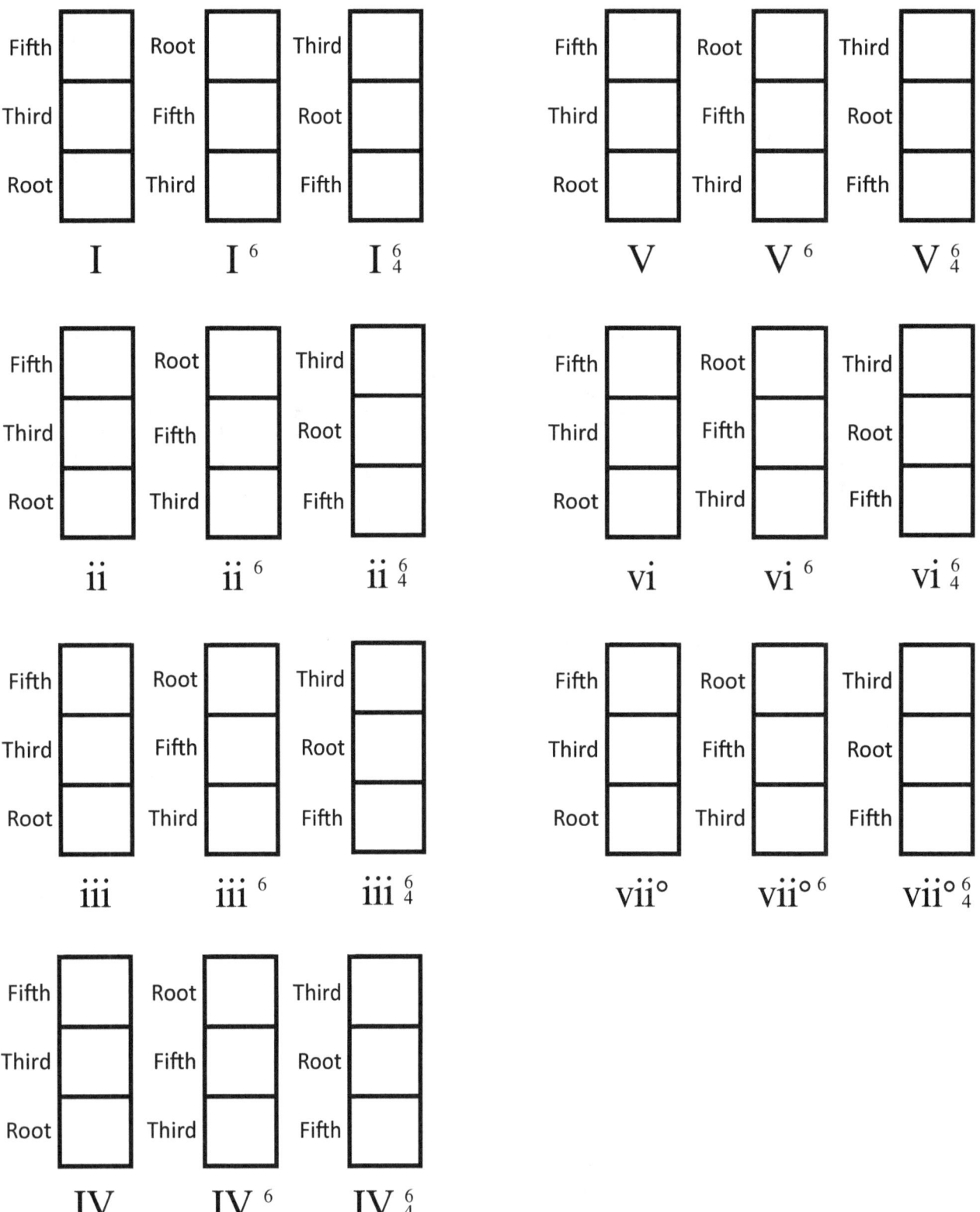

B♭ MAJOR

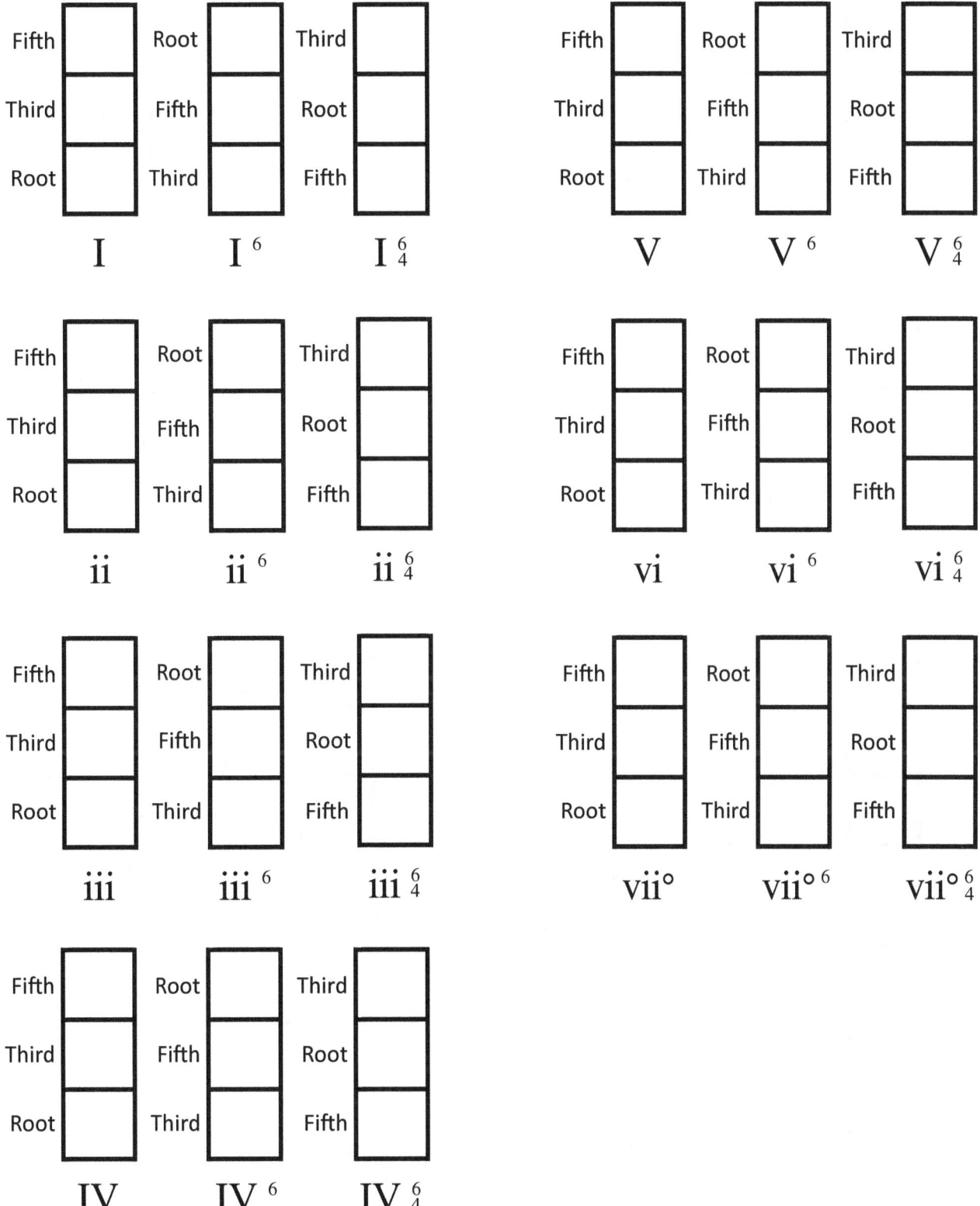

107

E♭ MAJOR

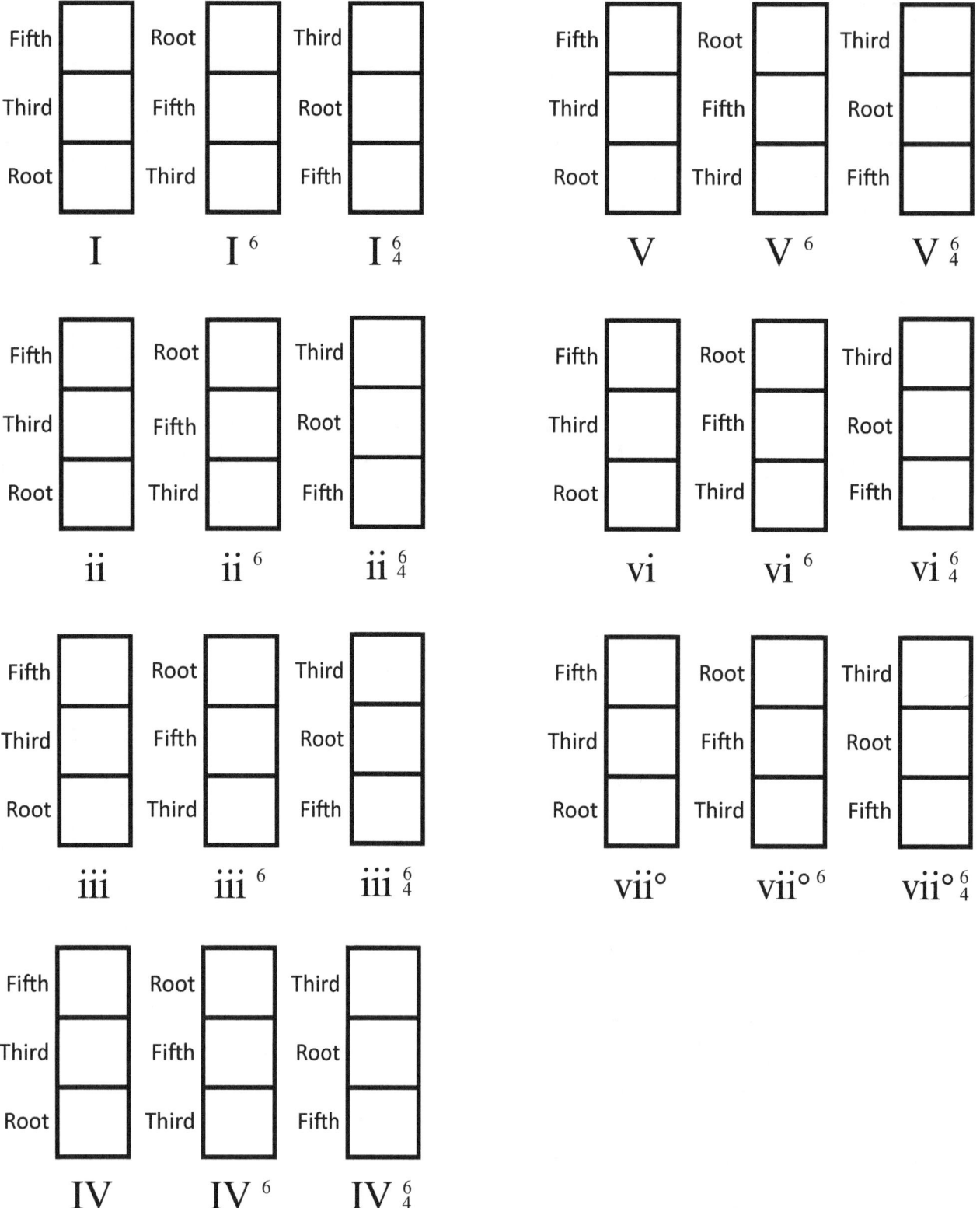

A♭ MAJOR

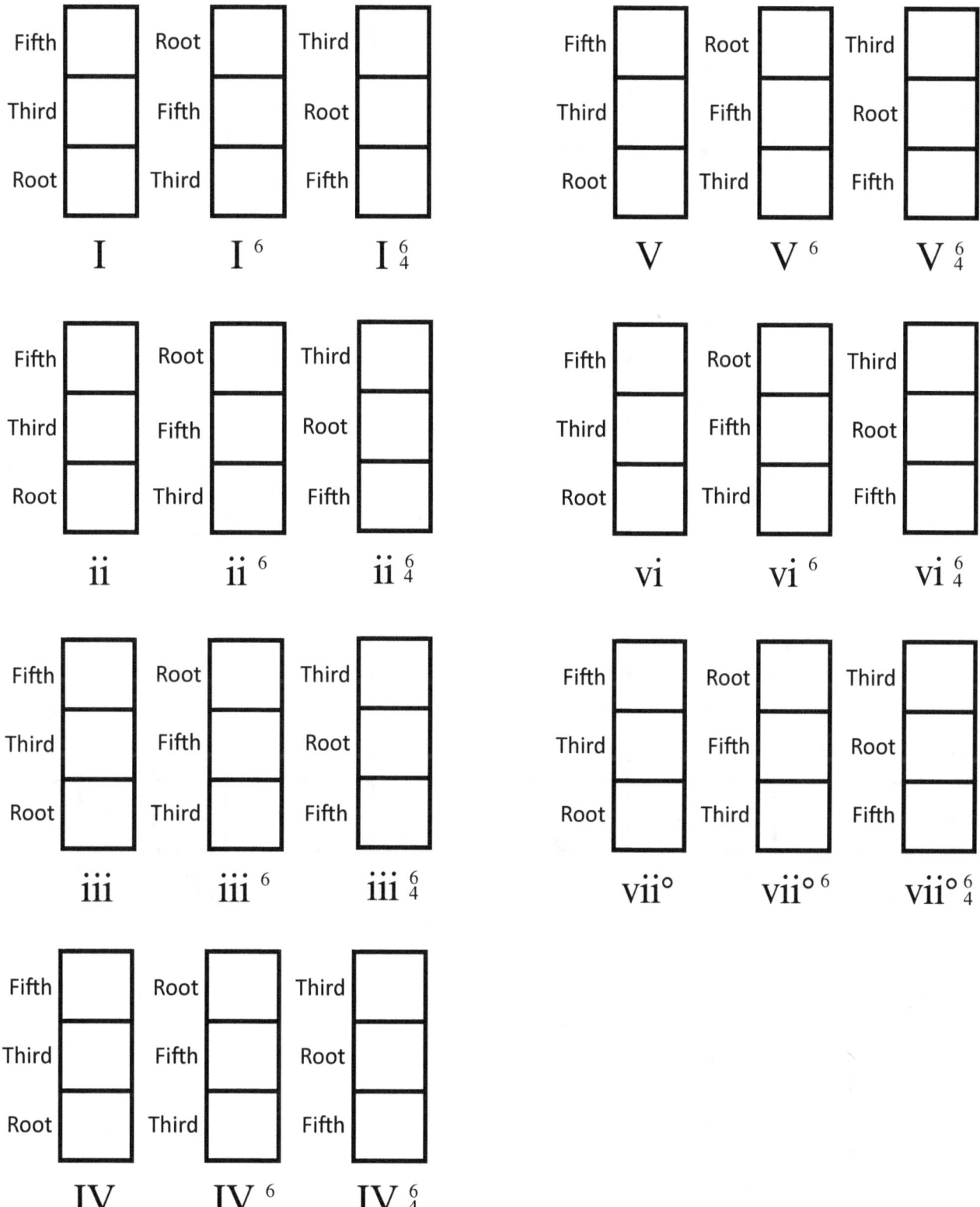

D♭ MAJOR

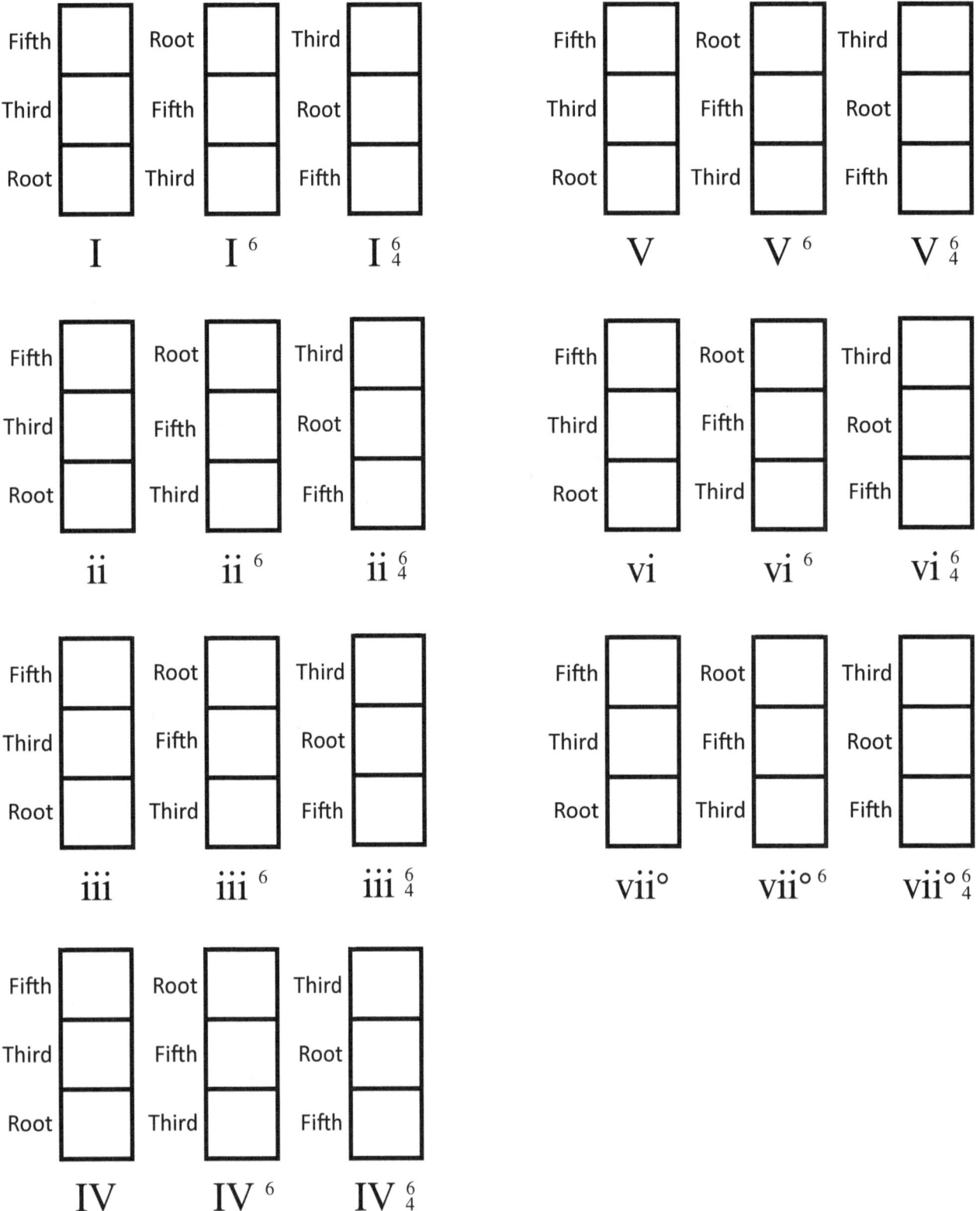

G♭ MAJOR

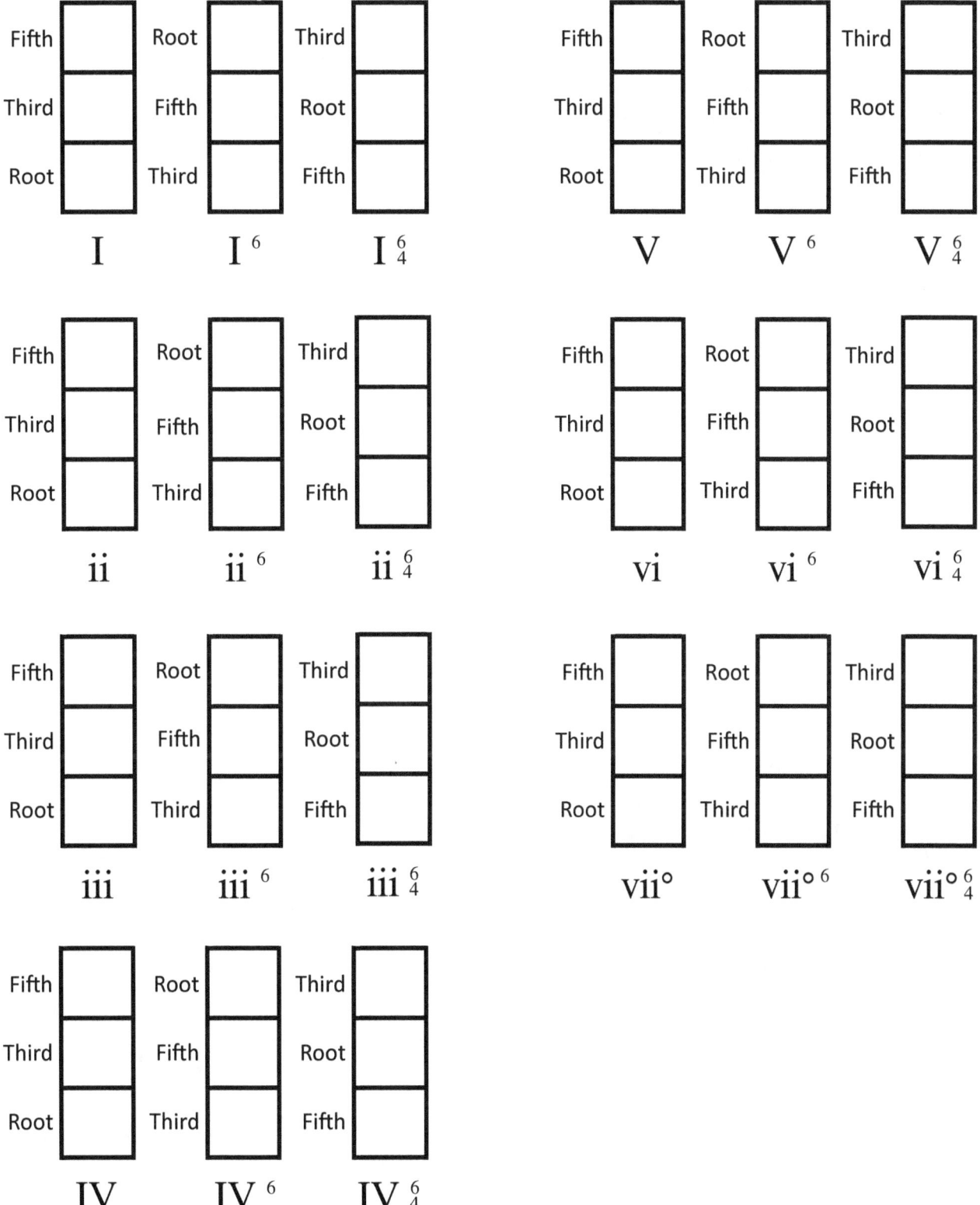

Enharmonic

Enharmonic refers to two notes that sound the same, but are spelled differently. C♯ & D♭ sound the same but are spelled differently.

In the examples below, can you identify the enharmonic key to the one given in the example?

MAJOR SCALES   **ENHARMONIC EQUIVALENT**

B Major   _____

F♯ Major   _____

C♯ Major   _____

B♭ Major   _____

E♭ Major   _____

A♭ Major   _____

D♭ Major   _____

G♭ Major   _____

C♭ Major   _____

F♭ Major   _____

V_7 Chords & Their Inversions

In each example, determine the correct V^7 chord (in root position) for the key given. Then label the root, third, fifth, and seventh of each chord. After that, use this information to write in the inversions. Here's a summary of the V^7 inversions.

First Inversion (V^6_5): Third on the bottom
Second Inversion (V^4_3): Fifth on the bottom
Third Inversion (V^4_2): Seventh on the bottom

C MAJOR

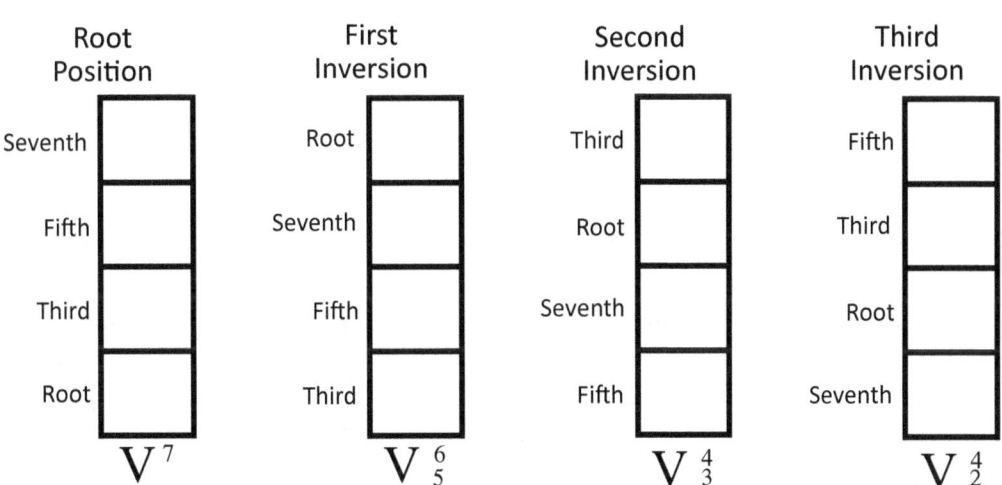

G MAJOR

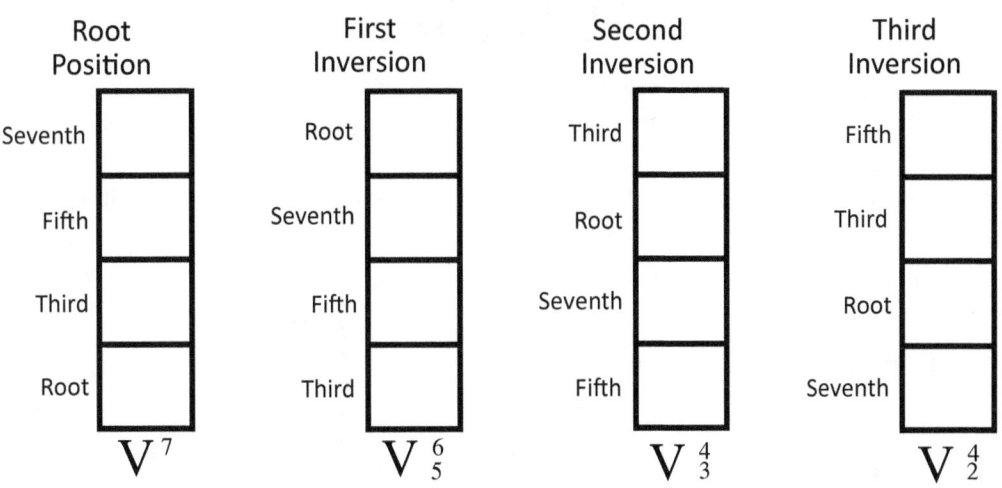

113

D MAJOR

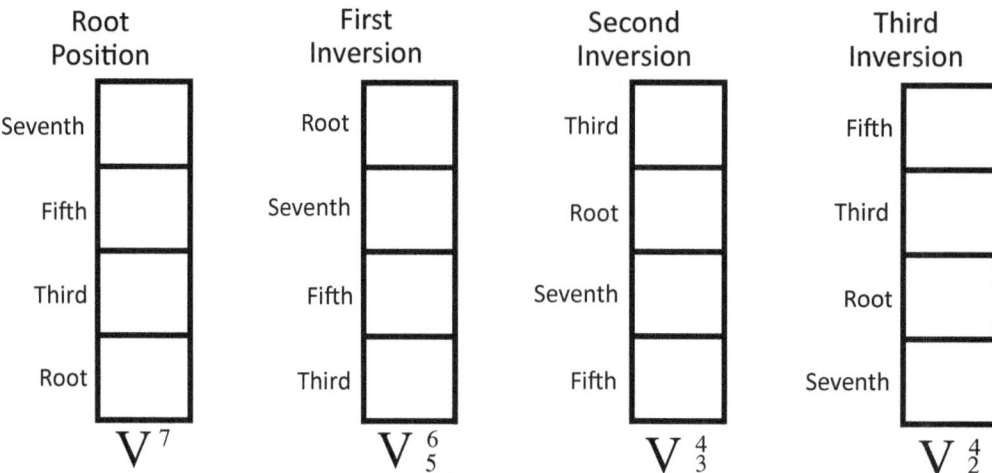

A MAJOR

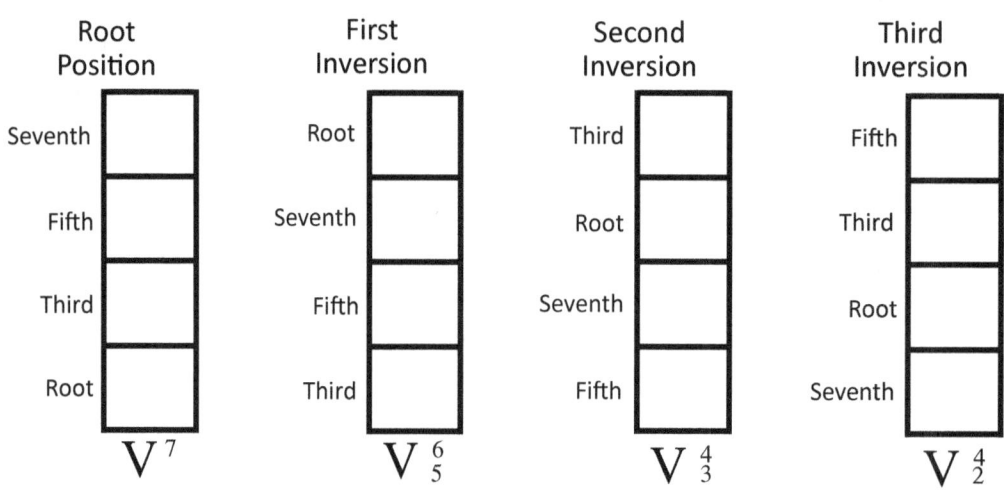

E MAJOR

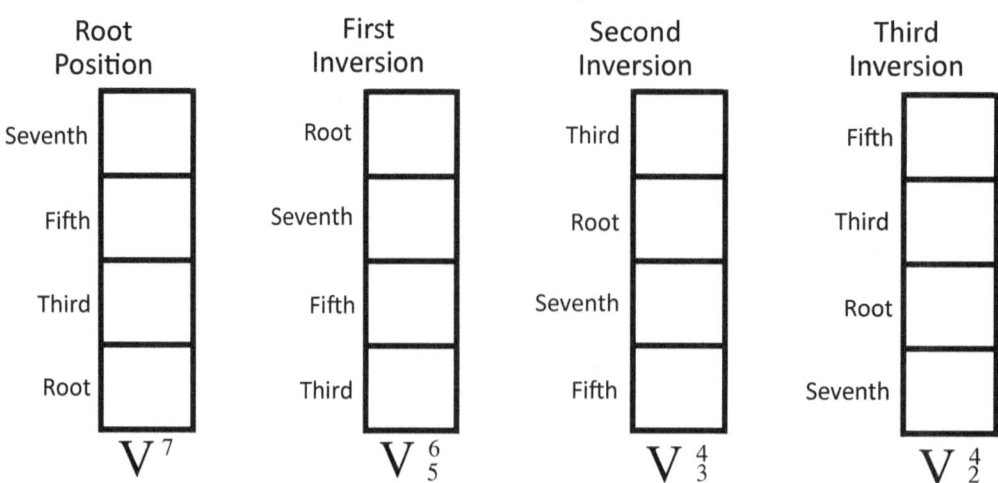

B MAJOR

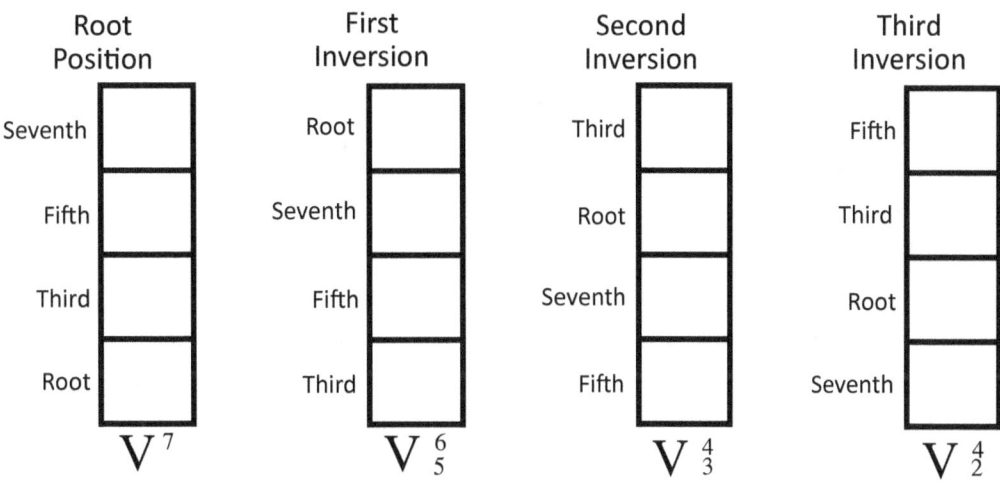

F# MAJOR

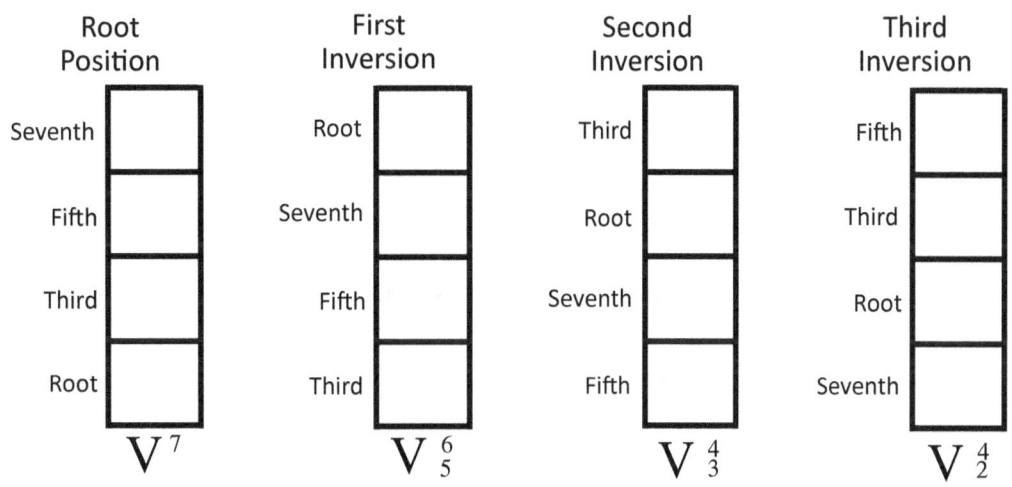

C# MAJOR

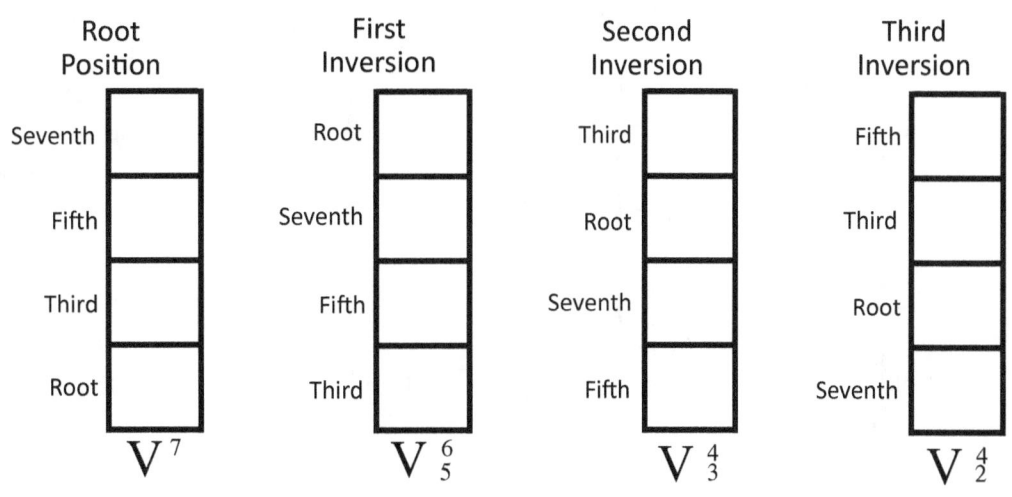

F MAJOR

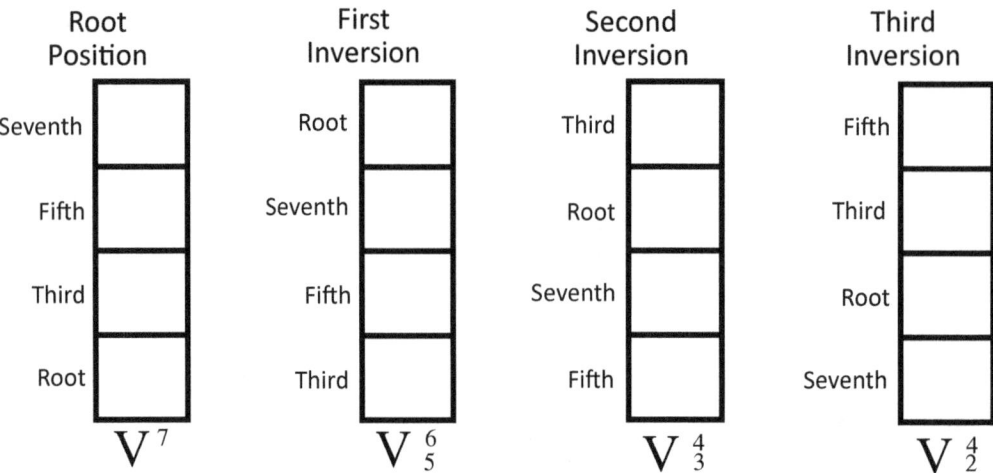

B♭ MAJOR

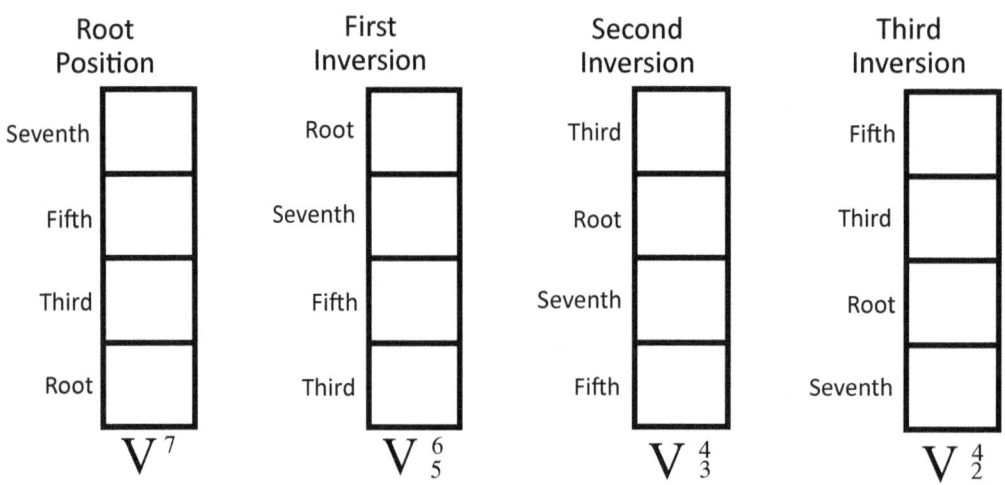

E♭ MAJOR

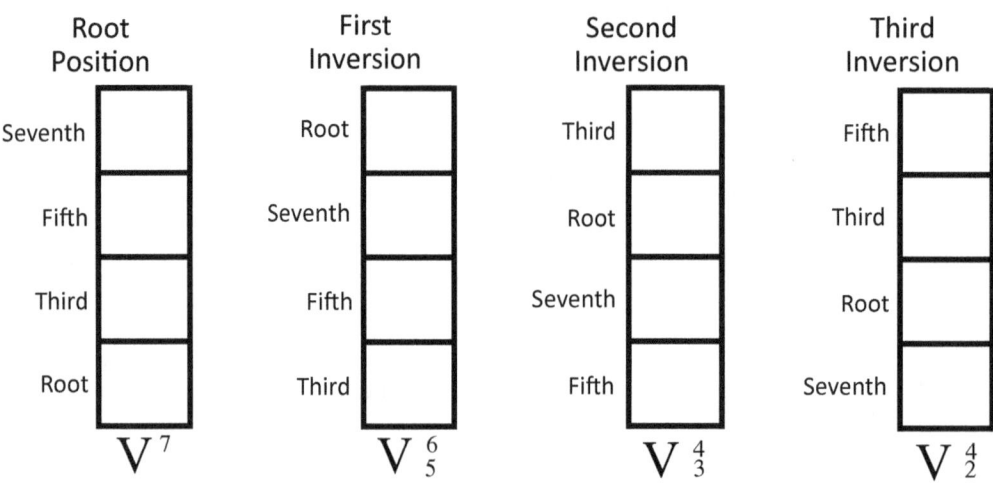

A♭ MAJOR

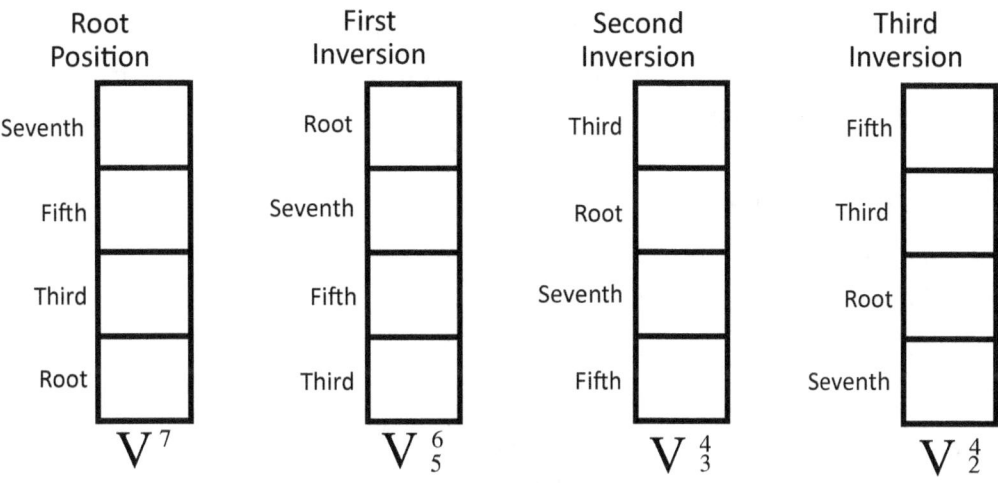

D♭ MAJOR

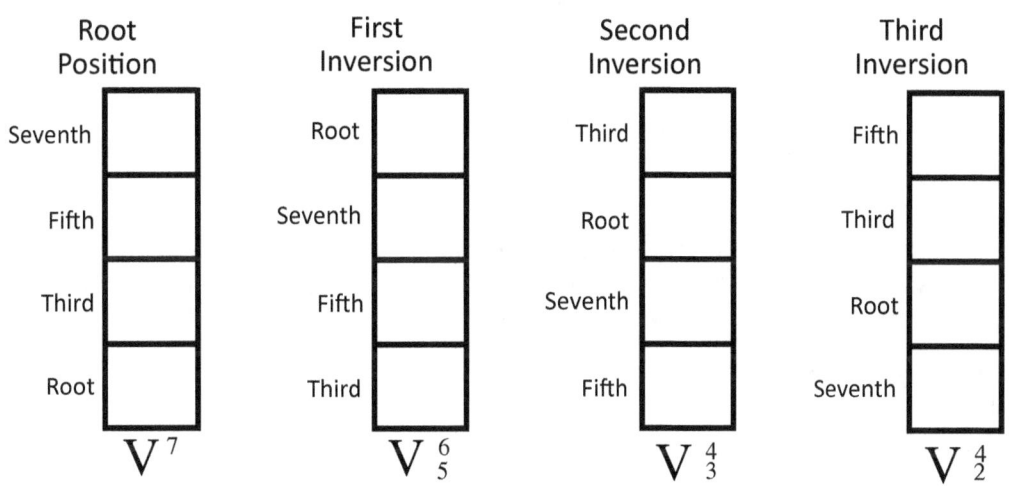

G♭ MAJOR

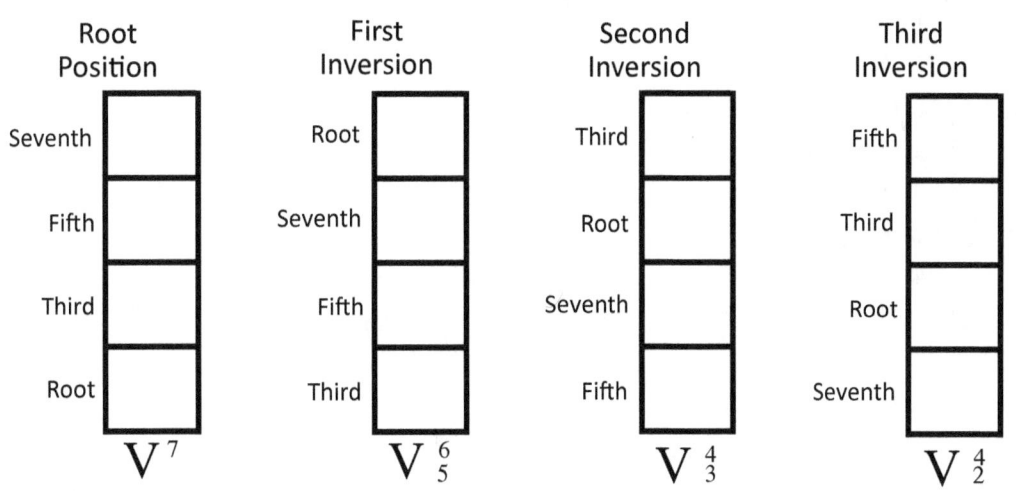

Suggestions For Learning Scales & Arpeggios

This last page provides some guidance and tips as you practice. There are many approaches to learning scales. You don't have to follow the suggestions below, but we at Maestro Music have found them to be effective in our studios.

Suggested Scale Fingerings

WHITE KEY SCALES: C-G-D-A-E
(Use the same fingering for Major & Minor Scales.)

RH 1 2 3 1 2 3 4 5 (Ascending)
LH 5 4 3 2 1 3 2 1 (Ascending)

For Descending: Play same fingering in opposite direction.
Clues for this Group: The 3rd fingers come together. The 4th Finger comes next to the Tonic.

B Major/Minor:
RH 1 2 3 1 2 3 4 5 (Thumbs on the white keys!)
LH 4 3 2 1 4 3 2 1 (Thumbs on the white keys!)
*For Left Hand, another common fingering is to only use thumbs on the white keys including "B."

F Major/Minor:
RH 1 2 3 4 1 2 3 4 (Note: You do not use your RH 5 finger in this scale!)
LH 5 4 3 2 1 3 2 1

BLACK KEY SCALES:
1) Notice you start and end on the same finger! This makes playing multiple octaves easier.
2) Many teachers will teach two different fingerings for these scales. However, you can use these fingerings for both major and all three minor scales.

F# (or Gb) Major/Minor:
RH 2 3 4 1 2 3 1 2
LH 4 3 2 1 3 2 1 4

G# (or Ab) Major/Minor
RH 3 4 1 2 3 1 2 3
LH 3 2 1 3 2 1 4 3

Bb Major/Minor
RH 4 1 2 3 1 2 3 4
LH 2 1 3 2 1 4 3 2

C# (or Db) Major/Minor
RH 2 3 1 2 3 4 1 2
LH 3 2 1 4 3 2 1 3

D# (or Eb) Major/Minor
RH 3 1 2 3 4 1 2 3
LH 2 1 4 3 2 1 3 2

Certificate of Achievement

This is to certify that

_____

has successfully completed
The Workbook, No. 2
of the Maestro Music Method.

Congratulations!

_____
Signed by Teacher   Date

www.ingramcontent.com/pod-product-compliance
Lightning Source LLC
Chambersburg PA
CBHW081200230426
43666CB00016B/2876